THE ACADEMY IV:

Title Fight

By T.Z. Layton

Books for Young Readers

This is a work of fiction. Names, characters, organizations, places, and events are either products of the author's imagination or are used fictitiously.

THE ACADEMY IV: TITLE FIGHT
Copyright © 2024, T.Z. Layton
All rights reserved.

No part of this book may be reproduced, or stored in a retrieval system, or transmitted in any form or by any means, electronic, mechanical, photocopying, recording, or otherwise, without express written permission of the publisher.

Published by First Touch Books for Young Readers
Cover design by Robert Ball
Interior by JW Manus

FOR TEMAI

Lewisham Knights

RETURNING PLAYERS

#10	Leo	United States
#11	Patrick	Ireland
#6	Otto	Hungary
#7	Ajay	India/England
#5	Riley	England
#4	Brock	England
#1	JoJo	England

NEWBIES

#8	Goran	Serbia
#9	Dmitri	Russia
#2	Kenji	Japan
#3	Emile	France/Cameroon
#12	Duncan	Scotland
#19	Marco	Colombia
#13	Ian	South Africa

SPECIAL GUEST APPEARANCES

John
Eddy
Sami

From the Journal of Leo K. Doyle

Note to Readers

Well, that was fun.

Traveling through Europe was one of the best experiences of my life. I can't wait to go back one day. Not in my wildest dreams could I have imagined we would win the Tournament of Champions, but somehow, it all came together on one amazing night in Paris. Things like that happen in sports, you know? Sometimes it's just your day.

When I returned home to Ohio, I was riding high. But I have a lot of work ahead of me on my journey to become a pro. My team has a lot to prove, too. Beating the Dragons at the end of last season was a great victory. But we still finished in next-to-last place. Can we find a way to win more games, manage the pressure that comes with success, and compete for a championship?

Being an underdog and winning a big game is one thing.

Taking on the champs all season long and coming out on top is another.

Plus, a lot changed over the summer. The Dragons have gotten even better, if you can believe that. In addition to their returning stars, like José and Diego, they added a few new players, some of the best in the world. One of them came from *our* team. You'll find out soon who decided to join our archrival.

Our team is changing, too. A few players have transferred, and some of my best friends moved on to the U16s. Almost half our team is gone. And the new recruits this year?

They're good players, no doubt about it.

But I don't know if they'll make us better.

One of them, Goran, is a center mid with a very different style from mine. He's big, tough, rough, and doesn't like me very much. In fact, he made it clear from day one that he's aiming for my position.

Worst of all, something bad happens to me during the season. I don't want to talk about it right now because I don't want to spoil the story. I'd rather give you all the details along the way, so you can form your own opinion. Let's just say I'm not sure I'll make it through the season or even be in the Youth Premier League next year. I'm starting this journal over Christmas break, and I don't know how it's all going to end.

I don't want to depress you or anything. This story is going to keep you on the edge of your seat. I've got a ton to tell you. About the new season and the new players, what's happening with all my friends, all the exciting games, and whether or not we'll be able to pull our team together and challenge the London Dragons for the title. Some of the other teams have improved as well. Anyone can win the league. Since I can't control the future, I'm going to take a deep breath, write a little more, and get back to practicing.

Let's see, what should I tell you first?

Yeah, I've got it.

Right where I like to start: Back home, on the field, in the thick of the action.

You better hang on tight.

ENTRY #1

The Calm Before the Storm

"Hey you! Yeah, you with the Knights jersey! Why don't you and your friend join the red pennies?"

I was the guy wearing a Knights jersey and my friend was Carlos. The person barking at us, one of the coaches at a summer skills clinic, had just put us in a group with the smaller kids. They were all in sixth and seventh grade and elementary school.

Though Carlos was a year younger, I was about to start eighth grade. The other players my age were grouped with the high school kids.

I understood. I was small for my age, a little below average height and as thin as a piece of spaghetti. As Carlos and I jogged over to join the younger kids, we grinned at each other, knowing what was about to happen. Even Carlos was too good for that group.

Let me back up. When I returned to Ohio after the Tournament of Champions, I still had a few weeks of summer left. Most of the time I spent with my friends, hanging out at the local pool and playing soccer in the park. Today—the first Saturday in August—I was attending a one-day clinic run by Chapman College, a private school about thirty minutes from Middleton. They have a good soccer team and play in NCAA

Division II. When I was younger, my parents took me to see them play.

My dad signed me up for the clinic, which surprised me. We never have money for things like that. Before I went to London, I'd never been to a single clinic or summer camp.

The head coach of the Chapman College Buccaneers, Coach Davis, was in charge. After he demonstrated a skill, we all returned to our groups, where the other coaches—mostly sophomores and juniors on the Buccaneers college team—helped us learn. It was all very basic compared to Samantha's practices. But hey, the more soccer the better.

Even though I took it easy and didn't want to show off, the coaches noticed pretty quickly I had talent. Eventually they moved me to the high school group. At the end of the day, Coach Davis thought it would be fun to have a short coaches versus players scrimmage. He picked eleven of the best players in the camp to scrimmage against the nine college players who were helping out. I was the only middle schooler picked to play, so Carlos had to watch from the sideline.

Coach Davis lined up our team and stuck me at right mid. I was the smallest player on the field. When the whistle blew, I decided to play hard since I was going against college players.

The Buccaneers passed the ball around for a while, laughing and doing tricks. They weren't taking us seriously, but it still took our team a while to get the ball. Once we did, we turned it over pretty quickly. Five minutes passed before I even had a touch. When I did receive a pass, I gave my right winger a sweet lob over the defense, but he bobbled the trap.

Soon after that, the coaches scored a goal. Our team kicked

off and worked the ball back to our keeper. I ran back, calling for the ball: "I'm open!"

The goalie slung the ball out. It went over my head and rolled into open space. I arrived a step before the opposing midfielder, poked the ball through his legs before he could get set, and ran around him. The college kids jeered their teammate that I had just nutmegged.

Another midfielder stepped up, standing up straight and facing me head on. Noticing he was not low and set like he should be, I feinted once, kicked the ball ahead, and blew past him.

Now I veered to my left, trying to get in position for a shot. The coaches only had nine players, so there was just one defender between me and the goal.

"Hit me!" one of my teammates cried, a left winger running on to goal.

The center back stepped up. We had a two v one, so a pass to my winger was the smart play. But the center back shifted in that direction, guessing too early. At the last moment, I pulled the ball back with the bottom of my foot, pushed it to the right, and drove forward.

The center back scrambled to catch up. I took two long dribbles, which took me right to the penalty spot, then blasted a shot into the bottom left corner, beating the keeper.

For a second, no one spoke. The coaches looked stunned. Then our team—and all the players watching on the sidelines—began whooping and cheering. Carlos was plucking at his hair as if he couldn't believe what had happened.

"Who's that guy?" someone yelled. "Move him to striker!"

Coach Davis followed the advice and moved me to center

forward for the rest of the game. I think the college players thought I had gotten lucky because they still didn't play very hard. But after I embarrassed another of them off the dribble and had a sweet assist for a second goal, they began marking me tight. After that, I had trouble beating them one v one because they were much older and twice my size. But I caused them all kinds of problems and they only beat us 3–2.

As I walked off the field, sweat pouring off my face, I noticed some of the college players pointing at me. I got a drink of water from a cooler on the sideline and went to meet Carlos. While we were talking, Coach Davis walked over. He was a fit and tanned man about my dad's age, wearing shorts and a T-shirt with the Buccaneers logo. His buzz cut had gray along the edges.

"Hey, guys," he said as he studied our name tags. "Leo and Carlos. Nice to meet you, boys. You're both excellent players. Are you from around here?"

"We're from Middleton," Carlos said.

"Ah, yes, not too far." He turned to me. "Leo, I have to say, I was impressed out there. You're, um, *really* talented. You turned some of my guys around!" He chuckled. "Greg won't live that nutmeg down for a while." He straightened his visor. "Listen, I'm sure another coach has beaten me to the punch, but on the off chance no one has, I'm curious if you've signed anywhere? I know you're still a bit young. I'm guessing you're a sophomore?"

"I'm in eighth grade. Well, almost."

Coach Davis couldn't seem to find his voice. "*Eighth grade?* I've never seen . . . well, I don't even know what to say. You're obviously too young to sign—aren't you? Maybe

I should check the rules. We've never recruited a middle schooler . . . anyway, don't worry about that. Maybe next year, your parents can give me a ring."

Carlos piped up before I could respond. "He already signed somewhere."

"Is that right?" Coach Davis said. "Can't say I'm surprised. Who's the lucky team?"

"Lewisham."

"Hmm. I'm not aware of that school. Where's it located?"

Carlos smirked. "London."

Coach Davis's eyes moved downward and then widened, as if noticing my jersey for the first time. "You mean that jersey is . . . Son, do you mean the *Lewisham Knights*? In the Premier League?"

"Yes, sir," I said.

He stuck out a hand. When I accepted the gesture, he began pumping my arm up and down. "Well, Leo, I'm really glad you came. I can see why they wanted you. You're a heck of a player."

"Thank you."

"I know it's a long road to the pros, and I wish you the best of luck. If for some reason that doesn't work out, and you decide to come home for college, please contact us. I feel confident saying I'll have a scholarship with your name on it."

All of a sudden, I had a suspicion why my dad wanted me to attend this camp—a backup plan, in case I didn't make it to the Premier League.

Sneaky Dad.

Coach Davis offered his hand to Carlos as well. "Good luck to you both. Carlos, I hope to see you back next summer, and

Leo, as much as I'd love to coach you, I'd rather see you on TV one day."

When Carlos and I got back to Middleton, we had dinner at his house and then rode our bikes to meet Dennis at a boba shop that had just opened. I ordered a lychee tea, a flavor I had tried in London. Dennis asked me what it was.

"It's good," I said. "Try it."

"But what *is* it?"

"I don't know. A sugary fruit or something."

Carlos rolled his eyes. "Leo's all sophisticated now. He probably likes bangers and mash and French food."

"Chocolate crepes," I said. "Yum. I miss them already."

Carlos waved a hand. "Whatever. And everyone knows that lychee is a fruit from Mexico. My uncle has lychee trees."

Dennis stuck with caramel, his favorite flavor, and Carlos ordered a pineapple smoothie.

We took our drinks to an open table on the patio. The night was warm and pleasant. I was sad to be leaving my friends but super excited to start the new season. In three weeks, I'd be back on a plane to London.

Carlos sucked a long drink through his straw and shook his head sadly. "I can't believe you're gonna miss out on eighth grade."

"I'm not going to *miss* it," I said. "I'm just doing it in England."

"You know what I mean. We could be kings of the school here."

Dennis snorted and crossed his thick arms. "You're just a seventh grader."

"Age is just a number." Carlos turned to me. "You're being a little selfish, you know. Think about *us*. Our school. Imagine if you played for the soccer team! We'd crush everybody. Why don't you come back for high school?"

"Weren't you the one who told me I had to get to the Premier League so I could bring you with me? So the three of us can live in an apartment in London or Barcelona?"

Carlos slurped his smoothie. "That's a good point. I'll have to think about my priorities. Ask me next year, and I'll tell you what to do."

I leaned back in my chair. "There's no guarantee I'll get to stay, you know. They cut people every year."

Carlos frowned. "Weren't you just MVP of the Tournament of Champions?"

"Yeah, but I'm only thirteen. A lot can happen before I get offered a schollie."

Dennis burped. "A schollie? What's that?"

"It's like this. Tig told me—"

Carlos interrupted me. "Is that the Dragons pro you keep claiming to know?"

"I do know him, and he plays for the U21s. So he's kinda pro."

"You're not making any sense."

"If you'll shut your trap and listen, I'll explain. Of course, getting to the adult Prem means you've *really* made it. But Tig said the first step to turning pro is getting a paid scholarship by the end of your U16 season in the Youth Premier League.

Then you can get paid to play soccer. Not a lot, but something, and it means the clubs are serious about you."

Carlos and Dennis nodded as they absorbed that information.

"Well," Carlos said, "you better get one of those."

"Every season counts, and it's a long way to the Premier League. Lots of academy players my age—most of them, really—don't make it to the pros."

"Really?" Dennis said. "What do you think this season will be like?"

"Hopefully better than the last one," Carlos said. "They came in next-to-last place."

"But they beat the Dragons in the last game."

"That was *one game*. The Dragons will probably destroy them this year."

Dennis flicked a piece of bright red hair away from his eyes. "Whose side are you on, anyway?"

Carlos shrugged. "I just tell it like it is."

"Will you let Leo answer?"

I was laughing at my friends, and happy they were following along with my team. As I thought about what to say, I scooped out the boba from the bottom of the cup and chewed it slowly. "Things will be different. I'll be a year older, but some of my friends are moving up to the U16s. We'll have new players, and the other teams will, too. It could be . . . I don't know." I looked up at the dark and moonless night sky, thoughtful, wondering if our team could hold on to some of the magic we had captured over the summer. "To be honest, I'm not sure what to expect."

The next morning, I woke up, yawned, and stood in front of the mirror on the back of my door. I was shirtless and flexed my arms in different positions, trying to see if they had grown.

Nope. Still a couple of wet noodles. I only had a few small pimples, so that was good, and my hair was still long and curly and golden-brown. I looked pretty much the same as I had when I showed up at the London Dragons camp last summer.

Which was a problem. If I was *too* undersized for my age, that could affect my soccer career. Yeah, I know Messi and lots of other players are tiny. It's true you don't have to be big in soccer. But every little bit helps, and if you're not the best athlete then you better have world class skills.

I wasn't asking for that much. Just a few inches of height and some arm muscles. Maybe a little chest hair, too. And bigger thighs. And calves. And shoulders. Is that so hard?

Some players are really good when they're young, but they don't continue to get better or don't get any faster or, I don't know, so many things can happen along the way to the pros. I was serious when I told my friends that every season counts.

I flexed a few more times, trying to bring out some muscles that might have been hidden, then sighed and went to check on Messi. I expected to find him standing on top of his tree and rolling his beady eyes, wondering why I was worrying so much.

Instead, I found him lying on his stomach on the floor of his cage, almost as if he was sleeping. *Huh*, I thought. Messi never sleeps during the day. Bearded dragons are diurnal and sleep more or less how we do: At night, when it's dark. Whenever I was in the room, he was usually active, trying to get my attention or teach me a lesson.

But not this time.

I took a closer look and noticed his hind legs were a little swollen, and his beard was black and flared. I'd never seen his beard flare except in anger. Was he mad about something? I knew I hadn't forgotten to feed him. Maybe I hadn't played with him enough over the break. I opened the cage and lifted him out, but he barely moved. His head shifted to look at me, but he didn't rise up on his hind legs, walk along my arm, or do any of the things he usually does. He just settled onto his stomach and lay there.

Confused, I observed him for a while and didn't notice a change in his behavior. His beard was still black. I did a little searching on my device and learned that a dark beard meant one of two things: anger or pain.

Oh boy. Feeling uneasy, I went to my dad, and he agreed to take Messi to the doctor.

"Well now," said Dr. Patel, one of the veterinarians at the Middleton Animal Hospital, as she set Messi on an operating table. Dr. Patel had shoulder-length dark hair, kind eyes, and dimples when she smiled. "I see what you mean, Leo. Your little guy isn't doing so well."

My dad was standing beside me. As Dr. Patel probed my lizard, I chewed on my lip and mumbled, "What do you think is wrong with him?"

"That's what I'm trying to see. Just hang on."

Messi looked so sad and pathetic lying there on his stomach. He could barely move and had no interest in the outside world. I just knew something was wrong. "Is he going to be okay?"

My dad put his strong hand on my shoulder. "Leo," he said gently. "Let her finish."

I kept fidgeting as the minutes passed. I love reptiles and have wanted one for a pet for as long as I can remember. My parents would never consider a snake, but my mom, a month before she died, convinced my dad to let me have a bearded dragon. Messi was the last thing my mom had ever given me, and it made him extra special. I couldn't bear the thought of losing him.

Dr. Patel took X-rays and drew some blood. Finally, she stood up straight. "I can't say for sure until the bloodwork comes back, but I'm almost certain that Mr. Messi here has metabolic bone disease. It's not uncommon with bearded dragons, but unfortunately, it can be quite serious."

I swallowed. "Can they . . . die from it?"

She nodded. "I'm afraid they can."

"What is it?" I whispered. "Is there anything we can do?"

"To put it simply, MBD is a lack of calcium in the body. This can happen from a variety of causes—not enough sunlight and poor nutrition being the main culprits. If a lizard's calcium is low, they'll pull it from their bones and other places to try to replenish it. That can lead to soft bones, tissue damage, and paralysis. Left untreated, it can be fatal."

I could barely form my next words. "Do you think he's going to . . . Do you think we brought him here in time?"

"It's too soon to tell. Before you leave, I'm going to give

you strict instructions on how to care for him, okay? It's very important to follow them every day."

I swallowed. "Okay."

After our visit, Dr. Patel gave us a box of calcium pills for Messi, a strict diet plan, and a syringe for vitamin D. As soon as we got home, my dad installed special UVB lighting from the pet store in Messi's tank.

Over the next two weeks, I stayed by Messi's side, checking on him all day long and even setting my alarm every four hours to make sure he was okay. I watched him eat, took his temperature, and talked to him. For the first week not much changed, and I worried he would get worse. But eventually, slowly but surely, he began to perk up. On the third Saturday in August, Messi finally climbed to the highest branch in his tree, turned his beady eyes my way, and flared his beard.

Like I said, bearded dragons are only supposed to show their beards when they're angry or in pain.

But I'm pretty sure Messi was giving me a victory cry.

"Whew," I said, picking him up and setting him on my bed. "I was worried about you."

He strutted back and forth, looking more like himself.

The next morning, he seemed even better, and we took him back to the vet. Dr. Patel said he was going to be fine! In fact, she said Messi was a very special lizard and had recovered faster than any bearded dragon she'd ever seen. I was proud of my warrior and felt as if a huge weight had lifted off my chest.

On the drive home, I sat in the back seat with Messi.

"You leave in three days, Leo," my dad said. "Are you ready? Don't you worry about Messi. I'll take good care of him while you're gone."

I had been worried about leaving. Would my lizard survive without me? The two of us locked eyes, and when his forked tongue flicked out and he reared up on his hind legs, I knew he was giving me a silent command. I stroked his back and gave a little nod.

"I'm ready," I said.

ENTRY #2

Reunions, Rumors, and Revelations

On a Tuesday in August so hot you could fry an egg on the sidewalk, I cradled the picture of my mom on my bedside table, said goodbye to Messi and Ginny and Aunt Janice, grabbed my suitcase, and hopped into my dad's truck. We drove all the way to Detroit for a direct flight.

Before I knew it, we were at the gate and my flight was boarding. My dad took me by the shoulders and said, "I don't like this very much."

"Me neither."

"Keep up your schoolwork, okay?"

"Will do."

"Stay out of trouble, listen to your coaches, and be careful in the city."

"Yep."

"Get to bed on time, don't do anything—"

"*Dad.* I'm thirteen now."

"I know, I know. You're a teenager, and this isn't your first rodeo." He swallowed and squeezed my shoulders. "I'm real proud of you, kiddo," he said softly. "Show them what you've got over there."

After saying goodbye, I took a deep breath, ran my thumb over the top of my lion's tooth necklace that was tucked under my shirt, and walked onto the plane, ready for my second season in the Youth Prem.

The flight took off at nine p.m. and landed in London at ten-thirty the next morning. This time, I slept through most of the journey, so I arrived at Heathrow Airport feeling refreshed and eager to start the day.

A Knights manager I'd seen around the Caravan—a bald Irishman in a tracksuit who helped out with the U21s—met me at the gate and took me through the city on the London Underground (remember, they call it the Tube).

The manager was nice and knows Tig really well. He said Tig would be their starting right winger this year and had a bright future ahead of him—as long as he chose soccer over being a world-famous DJ. He was kidding about that. I think.

As much fun as I'd had touring Europe, it felt good to be in London again. I could read the signs on the street and understand what most people were saying. And riding on the Tube felt like coming home. I loved the movie posters on the walls and the musicians performing in the tunnels and the energy from all the people. We passed familiar stops like Paddington, Tottenham, and Liverpool, which I realize now is *not* where Liverpool F.C. plays. That's in a whole different city.

At Whitechapel, we switched to the London Overground and watched the city pass by from a train that runs on an elevated track. The size of London took my breath away all over again. I hoped I got to explore more of it this year. The city is so awesome I didn't even mind the gray and drizzly weather.

At last, we arrived in Lewisham and walked ten minutes

to a tall iron gate at the entrance to the academy. I felt a tingle of pride when I looked up at the silver sign with black letters.

LEWISHAM KNIGHTS
PLAYER DEVELOPMENT ACADEMY

The manager dropped me off at the brick administrative building. Just like last time, when I checked in, an attendant handed me a manila envelope and a duffel bag with the club badge and my name on the side. "Welcome back, Leo," she said with a smile. "You're in the same room as last year."

I walked down the long hall lined with signed jerseys and emerged onto the sprawling grounds of the academy. Groups of players were knocking the ball around on the practice fields. With a grin, I remembered how nervous I'd been when I arrived last year, when I didn't know anyone and had no idea if I'd be good enough to play.

I didn't see any of my close friends, so I went straight to my square, four-story brick building with soot-blackened chimneys. Inside, I breathed in the musty air and noticed a new sign beside a door near the staircase.

Last year, the sign had read Mr. Luca, Player Development Manager. Now it read Mr. Anderson, Assistant Manager.

In the Prem, a coach is usually called a manager. So I guessed we had a new assistant coach. I wondered what had happened to Coach Luca.

In my room, I set the duffel bag on the bed and opened it right away, eager to see if our kit—that means our uniform— had changed. And it had. Our home jersey was solid silver with black lettering, while the away jerseys were orange with black-and-silver trim. I also had a new ball and more Knights swag: practice uniforms, hoodies, shin guards, water bottles, track suits, and a few other goodies.

Besides the new kit, something else had changed: My number.

For the new season, I was officially a 10.

Whoa.

Though I'd suspected Samantha would change my number, I hadn't been sure. I held one of the home jerseys in my hands, tracing a finger over the black number 10 on the back. I was the main playmaker for the team.

It felt good, but I reminded myself I'd taken the position from Caden last year. What if someone else returned the favor?

I opened the thick manila envelope and saw the new season schedule, the team rules, my school assignments, and some other boring stuff I didn't bother to read. The pre-season schedule was the same as last year: breakfast at seven, two long training sessions every day, and curfew at eleven.

The door burst open, a familiar voice roared "Yank!" and a group of players rushed into my room: Brock, Patrick, Otto, and Riley.

Brock picked me up in a bear hug and carried me halfway across the room. After putting me down, we all whooped and fist bumped. Well, all of us except Riley, who stood in a corner and tilted his head up as a greeting. But I knew he was glad to see me.

"About time you got here," Brock said. "You're the last one."

"Really? How long have you all been here?"

"Just a day," Otto said. His wavy brown hair was shorter than before, and a new pair of glasses with black rims made his owlish eyes look even wider. "But we all came from England or Europe, so it was an easier journey for us. All the returning players, that is."

I looked around the room in dismay. "This isn't it, right? We have some other players back?"

Patrick did a split on the floor and threw up his hands. "I'm here. Who else do you need?"

"Someone that can play defense," I said.

"Hey!" Patrick jumped to his feet and then chuckled. "Okay, Wacken Kraken, that's fair."

My Irish friend was wearing a Demon Slayer headband that held back his mop of bright red hair. I looked at all of my friends with a pang of jealousy. We'd only been apart for a month, but Patrick had grown an inch or two since the first time we had met and had gained a little weight. So had Brock and Otto. Riley looked even wirier than before, as if he hadn't been eating very much, but he was a little taller, and his rattail was longer.

Brock turned my desk chair around and sat on it backwards. He was wearing a Manchester United tank top that showed off his thick arms. "Ajay's here, too. He's probably studying in his room."

"School hasn't even started," I said.

Brock snorted. "Poor kid."

"JoJo's back, right?"

"Yeah, but she lives at home. And Taye's healthy again, but I heard he transferred to Chelsea."

I blinked. "What?"

"Probably didn't think he could beat out JoJo at keeper," Patrick added. "Which is true."

"And that's it," Otto said. "Only seven returning starters."

My head was spinning with all the news, and I started ticking off players on my fingers. "John, Eddy, Sami, Caden—they're all moving up to the U16s. Wait—did they all make the team?"

Brock and Otto exchanged glances. They must have some inside information, which didn't surprise me. Brock knew everything about our team and the Premier League, and Otto knew everything about, well, everything.

"John and Sami and Eddy made it," Brock said. "Caden didn't."

"Oh," I said quietly. Though Caden and I had started out enemies, we had smoothed things over during the Tournament of Champions. I respected him on the field and was stunned he'd been cut. But that's how tough it was to make it in the Youth Prem. "Did he go to another club?"

"Not sure."

"We should check up on him," I said. "So that's ten starters . . . who's left?" I snapped my fingers. "Aron. He's back, right?"

Riley hawked something in his mouth, and I thought he was going to spit right on the floor. Instead, he swallowed it—gross—and flung out a hand in disgust. "That 'angin bobbins traitor went to the Dragons."

My jaw dropped. "Wait—what?"

"You heard me. He's a turncoat, innit, and when we play him, I'm gonna flatten him good."

Brock didn't seem as annoyed. "Whatever," he said. "Happens all the time. The Dragons are still the best team in the league, and they recruited him away." He cracked his knuckles. "But, yeah, I'm gonna flatten him, too."

I knew it was silly, and I didn't *want* to join the Dragons anymore, but I felt a little hurt they had recruited Aron instead of me. They still didn't want me! Maybe they saw more long-term potential in him.

My dad's voice popped into my head. *Stop worrying about things you can't control, kiddo.*

Brock stood and began to pace. "Aron isn't the only player they picked up. They got another transfer—one of the top fullbacks in the world—and I'm sure their new recruits are crackin' good, too. And they brought in a new coach from Argentina who's won championships in Spain and South America."

"Ouch," I said. "They're gonna be really tough."

"Maybe unstoppable," Otto added.

Patrick thew a pillow at him. "Luckabucka, Otto, don't be such a downer."

"I just state the facts as I see them. Notice I did not say *definitely* unstoppable. Just *maybe*. And their number one priority will be revenge against us for spoiling their perfect season."

Patrick rolled his eyes and saluted him. "Thank you, Captain Negative. Listen, alley cats, I gotta run. Smell you later."

Riley and Otto left too, leaving me and Brock alone.

"What about our new players?" I said. "Have you heard anything? Oh—and where's Coach Luca? Who's the new assistant?"

"Mr. Luca transferred, too. Picked up a head manager gig in Italy. Third division, but it's a good opportunity. I haven't met our new coach, but my dad says he's a former Premier League player—"

"Really?"

Brock looked amused. "Yeah, Yank, so are most of the managers in the Youth Prem. Anyway, he's been coaching in Serbia, and he brought his two best players with him: a striker and an attacking midfielder. They're both supposed to be top notch. Some new defenders came in, too. A Scot and two others. So we'll all have competition for playing time."

"I guess so," I said, wondering just how good the new players were, especially the attacking midfielder.

Brock rubbed his belly. "Time to feed the beast. See you in the canteen?"

Sometimes the English call a cafeteria a canteen.

"Yeah," I said, reeling from all the changes in the team. I wouldn't have John to pass to up front, or Caden in the middle, or the steady presence of Eddy and Sami in the back. "See you there."

Later in the day I had dinner in the cafeteria, where I caught up with Ajay for the first time since the end of last season. With a sigh of relief, I noticed he had barely changed, except for a pair of glasses he wore to dinner. He was about my height and even skinnier, which hardly seemed possible. He still talked really fast and was a little goofy, and some part of his gangly brown body was always moving or twitching, as if he had energy to burn.

After dinner, we all moved to the lounge, where we had an air hockey tournament and played a little FIFA. My long flight and jetlag began to catch up with me, so I went to bed a little early, tired but full of anticipation.

Tomorrow was the first day of practice, and I couldn't wait to get on the field.

ENTRY #3

Old Tests and New Teammates

Seven-thirty a.m.

Dew on the ground, crisp morning air, stray clouds in the sky.

Let's play!

After breakfast, I walked outside with my friends, laughing and joking but keeping an eye on the twelve new players, wondering who would make the first team and challenge us for our positions.

When we reached our practice field, I noticed Samantha on the sideline, chatting with a man in his thirties with a clipboard and a whistle around his neck. He was tall and square-jawed and looked very fit.

Brock nudged his head in the man's direction. "That's the new coach."

I caught Samantha's eye and waved. She smiled and waved back. Soon she blew the whistle and asked everyone to take three warmup laps. As I rounded the first corner flag, I noticed a familiar face with purple hair and pasty white skin sprinting towards the field. JoJo was wearing the same black goalie pants with silver lightning bolts down the sides she had worn during the Tournament of Champions. Knowing she was a little superstitious, I doubted she would change them unless we stopped winning.

Both Samantha and Coach Anderson frowned at JoJo's late appearance.

"Hope you didn't get a big head from that MVP award," JoJo said as she passed me on the second lap, then sped up before I could think of a good comeback.

When the warmup laps were finished, everyone took a knee in front of Samantha. She was wearing silver shorts, Adidas flats, and a black Knights sweatshirt. As usual, her long brown hair was tied in a ponytail. "Welcome back, everyone. It's good to see all the familiar faces as well as the new ones. I look forward to getting to know each one of you better over the course of the season. And hey—congrats again on winning the Tournament of Champions. I saw the final on TV and believe me, I was jumping up and down. Let's go, Knights!" She shook a fist in the air, and our team broke into cheers.

After we quieted, Samantha steepled her fingers against her mouth. "That was a great win for the club, and I'm so proud of everyone. But we've got a lot more to accomplish, don't we? Who wants to take that momentum and win the Youth Premier League this year?"

This time the cheering was even louder. On the next field over, the U18s stopped practicing to see what the commotion was about.

Samantha turned and opened a palm towards the man beside her. "I'd like to introduce Coach Anderson, who's here to help us do that. He used to play for Fulham and brings a wealth of experience."

There was a ripple of excitement at this news. Fulham's

a Premier League team. From the looks of our new coach, his young face and muscular thighs and calves, he hadn't retired all that long ago. I wondered if it would be awkward for Samantha to have an assistant ten years older than herself. Then I thought of the games I'd seen on TV, and all the coaches on the sidelines, and realized it happened all the time.

"Good morning, everyone," Coach Anderson said in a British accent. "I was standing in your shoes once and still remember my own academy days like they were yesterday. I hope I can live up to the standards my managers set. You all look ready and eager, so let's get on the pitch and start training. Oh, and I second the congrats on the tournament. That was an impressive run."

Though he seemed nice enough, his voice was stiff and businesslike. Maybe he'd loosen up after he got to know us.

"We've got a ton of work to do, Knights," Samantha said. "I assure you the Dragons and all the other teams are training harder than ever. After our recent success, we'll have a target on our backs. Our first game is less than a month away. That doesn't give us much time. We need to get you fit and figure out who our starters are."

When she said this, I noticed one of the new players, a sturdy kid with a low forehead and clipped dark hair, eying me from the opposite end of the semicircle. He was just as big as Brock and had hairy legs and forearms. I even saw a few chest hairs poking out of the top of his practice jersey. *This guy is thirteen?*

When I caught him looking, he met my eyes with a challenging stare. A little annoyed—*Who does this newbie think he is?*—I returned my attention to Samantha.

"Because I don't know all of you," she was saying, "we're going to run through a few performance tests. You can't fail," she said with a smile, "because you've already made the team. Think of it as a mini academy camp packed into one day. Tomorrow, we'll scrimmage to see how everyone looks in a game. I'll warn you, Knights. It's going to be a tough week. I need you to rest up, eat right, and show up every day with the right attitude, prepared to work hard. Okay?" She clapped and pointed to a corner flag. "Let's get our blood pumping with three Carolinas."

Ugh. This was my least favorite exercise. A Carolina is a single lap around the field as fast as you can go. It was short enough to almost be a dead sprint, and long enough to make you want to throw up when it was finished. After the first one, I almost did. I was out of shape from goofing off the last few weeks. That was okay. I believed in enjoying my time off as much as possible.

After the Carolinas, most of the returning players looked as exhausted as I felt. On the last one, I beat Patrick and JoJo by a hair, and Brock and Otto by a lot. Those two were huffing and puffing towards the rear. Riley and Ajay could run like gazelles, and they were at the front with three newbies: Dmitri, a lean player with spiky, bleached blond hair and a cocky sneer; a handsome, dark-haired guy named Marco; and Kenji, a Japanese kid who pushed himself to the very edge to come in first. As soon as he finished, he leaned over and threw up on the field, then apologized to Samantha.

"It's fine, Kenji," she said. "The grass will survive. You don't have to kill yourself though. Push hard but save some energy."

"Yes, Coach Samantha," he said in a thick accent. "This I will promise to do."

Some of the new players chuckled at his English, but Samantha silenced them with a heavy stare. I guessed this was Kenji's first time overseas, or at least in an English-speaking country. In addition to competing at the highest level of soccer, he had to learn a whole new language and set of customs.

"Thank you," Samantha said sweetly to Kenji. "Okay, everyone. Take a break and meet me back here."

As I guzzled water on the sideline, Brock came over holding his sides and breathing hard. "Too . . . many . . . chips . . . this . . . summer."

"Me, too," I said. Chips meant French fries in England. "And banana pancakes, and chicken wings, and chocolate chip cookies."

"Yeah," Otto said, wiping sweat off his large forehead. "Who invented Carolinas anyway? A medieval torturer?"

During the water break, Coach Anderson set up cones all over the field. When we returned to Samantha, she led us through a stretching session, then asked everyone to line up by one of the goals.

"Two sprints," she said. "End line to end line. Three minutes of rest in between. Let's see who our speedsters are!"

When the whistle blew, I took off as fast as I could. Only three players beat me: Riley, Dmitri, and Ajay. Riley and Dmitri were neck and neck for first place, and Samantha declared it a tie. Ajay beat me by a hair.

"That new guy's fast," I said to Otto, talking about the player with spiky blond hair and a cocky sneer who had tied Riley. "Is he a nine?"

"Correct. Dmitri's Russian but he played in Serbia with Goran and Coach Anderson."

"Who's Goran? The big guy with chest hairs who looks about sixteen?"

"That's the one."

"So, Dmitri . . . can he score?"

"He had the second most goals in the league," Otto said. "Serbia isn't the Premier League, but you never know where the best players might come from. Some people grow up in the middle of nowhere."

Yeah, I thought. *Like me.*

Next up was pushups and sit-ups. I didn't like those any more than I had during the Dragons summer camp. I promise you I will *never* like them.

I came in last on the pushups. How embarrassing. I caught Coach Anderson frowning at me, which made me feel guilty. Brock and Goran tied for the most. They almost did seventy each. Seventy!

I was terrible at sit-ups, too, though I was relieved to see a skinny newbie named Emile complete even fewer than I did.

Duncan, a Scottish fullback built like John—a fire hydrant with arms and legs—came in third in both exercises. One of the new goalies, a tall kid with sandy hair named Ian, was right behind him.

During the next water break, the guys roasted me for my performance. I waved it off, pretending it didn't bother me. "Whatever. Give me a ball and we'll see what happens."

⚽ ⚽ ⚽

Remember the high jump test from the Dragons Academy? The portable pole with plastic markers every inch up to twelve feet? Coach Anderson wheeled one onto the field. Although Patrick isn't the tallest player, he jumped the highest, and touched nine and a half feet!

JoJo came in third, which didn't surprise me. Marco, the dark-haired newbie a little taller than Patrick, finished second.

"Who's that guy?" I asked Otto again, who seemed to know every player in every youth league in Europe.

Surprisingly, Otto wasn't sure, but a voice from behind us said, "Marco's a baller, eh?"

I turned and saw Emile. He was very slight like me, and his head was long and narrow. But he had a charming smile—cocky, even—and a presence about him that made him seem bigger than he was. His skin was like caramel, light brown and smooth, and his hair was cut right to his scalp. He told us he was born in Cameroon but had lived around the world because his mother was a French diplomat.

In fact, he told us so much about himself that I finally stuck out my fist and said, "I'm Leo."

Emile seemed amused, and his eyes flicked to my jersey. "I can read, eh?" He spoke very good English. "Marco and I were teammates at Olympique."

"Ah," Otto said. "I don't follow Ligue 1 very much, except for PSG."

"Our team just played in Paris," I said.

"Yeah. I know." Emile seemed amused again that I had told him another obvious fact. But how could I know if he kept up with the Tournament of Champions?

"You were the MVP," he continued, looking me up and

down with a doubtful expression, as if he had trouble believing I had won the award. He turned back to Otto and said, "Where do you play?"

"Normally the eight. Midfield."

"I know what an eight is."

"What about you?" Otto asked.

"Fullback, wingback. Not like Duncan though." He rolled his eyes in the direction of the Scottish newbie. "I'm a modern player. I like to invert, eh?" He could tell I had no idea what he was talking about. "You know, like Cancelo and Zinchenko."

Nope. Still no idea. I knew who those players were, but I wasn't sure what he meant by invert.

"Inverted fullbacks like to drift inside and help in midfield," Otto said. "Provide more passing options and help the team keep possession. They have to be really good on the ball."

"Ah," I said.

Emile nodded at Otto. "You know your football. Anyway, Marco's a winger from Colombia. Doesn't say much, but he can play. A straight cold assassin. We're lucky to have him. When Coach Anderson recruited me, I told him he should take Marco, too, if he knew what was good for him."

Somehow I doubted that Emile was the one who had convinced the Knights to sign Marco.

As Samantha waved everyone over, Emile made a V with two fingers on each hand and pointed them at us. "Good luck, chaps. Hopefully we'll get on the pitch soon. These tests are for the birds."

As he jogged back, I almost said, *You finally said something I agree with*, but I held my tongue. Better not to make enemies on the first day.

Next came the agility tests. You probably remember these, too. At last Samantha rolled out a ball, and on the first test, we wove through a line of cones all the way down the field and back. I did well—a second-place finish each time, just a step ahead of Emile. Patrick came in first, which led him to do a back flip and shoot an arrow towards the main stadium.

"Save it for the games, Patrick," Samantha said with a grin.

Not far behind me, Marco and Riley finished in a tie, straining to edge each other out. Goran and Dmitri came next. Dmitri was blindingly fast but didn't have the best ball control. Ajay sprinted through after him, and his dribbling was even worse. Then Otto huffed and puffed across the line. Further back was Ian, who had good foot skills for a goalie. He could dribble as well as all of our defenders except Emile, who controlled the ball like a midfielder.

JoJo came in last and made us all laugh by complaining loudly about the goalies having to dribble.

Well, everyone laughed except Coach Anderson, who was frowning again, though I wasn't sure why.

If I'd been in better shape, I was pretty sure I would have won that race. But the last one was my favorite. Coach Anderson set up a line of cones twenty yards long and much closer together. We had to weave through them with the ball as fast as possible, cutting hard like we were going around defenders.

I didn't just win. I beat everyone with room to spare.

"Very good, Leo," Samantha murmured as I crossed the finish line.

Emile finished second, Patrick came in third, and Goran

came in fourth. It was intimidating watching someone that big travel side to side so quickly, like a boss from a video game moving across the screen.

Samantha called for another break. As I gulped down a cup of water, Duncan, the new Scottish fullback, walked over. He had red cheeks, large ears, and a young-looking face with short brown hair combed to the side, the sort of haircut a little kid would have. He also tucked his shirt in tight, like his parents had dressed him. I doubted he had turned thirteen. But he had thick strong legs and performed well in all the tests.

He introduced himself and congratulated me on the MVP award over the summer. "You're *really* quick with the ball," he added.

"Thanks," I said, feeling my head grow a few sizes. Duncan's accent was so thick I had trouble understanding it. "Where are you from?"

"I'm Scottish," he said, without pronouncing the t's. "From Edinburgh."

"Oh. What's that like?"

He considered the question. "Cold. Nice. Very old buildings." I thought he was done speaking, but he said, "You're from the States, right? I've never met anyone from there. Well, a few tourists." He cocked his head to the side. "Come to think of it, I haven't met anyone from anywhere."

Right away, I could tell a couple of things about Duncan. He was friendly, he said what was on his mind, and he was a little naïve about the world outside his home.

Sort of like me when I arrived at the London Dragons summer camp.

"Where'd you play before this?" I asked.

"In the Scottish League. Philip Niles scouted me."

"Really? Me too! So you must be *really* good."

He blinked as if he hadn't gotten the joke. Maybe we weren't exactly the same.

"What are the coaches here like?" he asked. "My old coach made us run at six in the morning every day. I kind of liked it though. I'm an early riser."

Okay, maybe we weren't similar at all.

"That sounds . . . pretty terrible," I said. "Samantha's the best, but I don't know anything about Coach Anderson."

"I guess we'll find out."

A whistle blew, and we jogged back on the field with the others.

⚽ ⚽ ⚽

For the rest of the day, we ran through the basics: shooting, passing, trapping, heading, and defense. The coaches watched carefully and took notes on their clipboards.

I won't bore you with the details of every single drill. It was a lot like the first few days at the Dragons Academy, except this time, I knew what I was doing.

As we went through the stations, everyone kept an eye on everyone else, trying to see how good they were. First up was shooting. When Coach Anderson demonstrated the proper technique, I could hardly believe how powerful his shot was. At Fulham, he was a defensive midfielder, but he had scored a few goals during his career. When he hit the crossbar, I thought it might crack.

Samantha was a striker, and her shot was even more accurate than Coach Anderson's. Not to mention she has moves that would make your jaw drop.

Who impressed me most among the players?

You might think our forwards had the best shots. And they were pretty good, especially Patrick. He was consistent and tricky. Dmitri could kick hard but wasn't very accurate. And Ajay, well, his shot needed work. (Remember, I'm judging everyone by Youth Premier League standards.)

But our midfielders shot just as well. My own technique was excellent now, and Goran had a cannon for a leg. He could score from thirty yards out. His passing was amazing, too. He couldn't dribble as well as me, but I had to say he impressed me with every other skill.

What else?

Marco had a wicked cross from the right wing, much better than Ajay's.

Emile had a great first touch and slick moves for a defender.

Duncan was a sneaky good player.

One of the newbies, the Japanese defender named Kenji, was still a mystery. He was quick and fast and threw his body around like he didn't care about an injury. But I would have to see him play in a game to judge him better.

Which I would get to do very soon. As we all trudged off the field at the end of practice, exhausted and pouring sweat, I could tell that everyone, like me, felt unsatisfied. Sort of like we'd been riding a bike at slow speed instead of flying down a hill, the wind in our faces.

Drills were one thing, games were another.

It was time to see who could play.

ENTRY #4

Starters versus Newbies

The morning arrived before I knew it. After breakfast and warmups, I lined up in midfield with my teammates, ready for a scrimmage. We were playing a full game with forty-five-minute halves. Coach Andersen was the referee.

I thought Samantha might select a few of the best newbies to join the returning starters. But she didn't, and I should have known better. Samantha makes her players earn their starting spot, just like when she put Aron on the second team to start the summer.

All the returning starters were on my team: Patrick, Otto, Brock, Riley, JoJo, and Ajay on the right wing.

On the other side, Samantha had selected the best newbies to start: Dmitri at striker, Marco on the right wing, Goran opposite me in center midfield, Emile and Duncan at fullback, and Kenji holding down the defense at center back. Ian, the tall South African kid with big hands and sandy hair, was in the goal.

The first game was less than a month away. All the newbies wanted to make a good impression, and we starters wanted to lock down our positions.

This was going to be interesting.

Samantha blew the whistle. Our striker passed to me to start the game. I sent the ball to Otto, who faked a pass to Patrick and returned the ball to me. Goran was coming on hard. I put my first touch into a pocket of space, beat Goran to the spot, and slipped a pass to Ajay down the wing. Right after I made the pass, Goran plowed into me from behind, causing me to face plant on the ground.

Ouch. The whistle blew, signaling a foul. I pushed to my knees and found a hand waiting to help me up. It was Goran. "Sorry," he mumbled in a voice that did not sound sincere.

So that's how it's gonna be, I thought.

I accepted his hand, brushed grass off my uniform, and took the free kick, curling a beautiful pass to Patrick as he cut inside. Patrick rose for a header and flicked it across the box, where Ajay was streaking inside. He tried a half volley that missed the goal and everything else in South London.

"Keep your head down," Samantha called out to Ajay. "Eyes on the ball."

A little sheepish, Ajay nodded and hustled back. I could tell he was rusty.

This time, the newbies worked the ball downfield. Kenji took the goal kick and passed to Duncan on the right. When Patrick pressured him, Duncan chipped a ball across the field to Emile. The left fullback settled the ball nicely and headed upfield. As Ajay stepped up to defend, Emile opened his hips to pass, then rolled the top of his foot over the ball, carrying it to the side. He slid by Ajay and continued upfield.

A slick move, I had to admit.

But a risky one. If Emile had lost the ball from that position, it could have cost them a goal.

Samantha had the same thought. As Emile made a long

pass down the sideline, she called out, "Too much, Emile. Make the simple pass."

After Samantha turned away, I noticed Emile rolling his eyes.

The pass almost slipped through, but Riley took a gamble, raced upfield, and intercepted it. Riley used to be a forward and had pretty good foot skills. He took two dribbles and passed to me in the center. When the ball arrived, I turned, just barely redirecting the ball with the bottom of my foot. Now I was facing our opponents' half, where I saw Goran coming on hard.

But I also saw Patrick and Ajay streaking down the wings. I lofted a pass over the top of the defense. Patrick chested it near the edge of the penalty box. Before the ball touched the ground, he struck a hard volley that screamed towards the top left corner.

Ian crouched on the goal line. As the shot came in, he took a few steps and leaped high. He had big, long arms and managed to push the volley away with his fingertips. But the ball hit the side of the goal and bounced back into the penalty area, where Patrick was waiting. He was smart and had followed his own shot. Before Ian could recover, Patrick slipped an easy pass into the goal.

Returnees 1, newbies 0.

Soon after the kickoff, Otto intercepted another pass. He shielded Goran long enough to send the ball to me. I one-touched the ball to our left midfielder, who was forced to turn and pass to the defense. Brock thought he had plenty of time, but Dmitri sprinted back to press him. Wow, Dmitri was fast. Brock barely had time to get off a pass. And Dmitri kept going, chasing after Riley as well.

As the Russian striker closed in, Riley pushed the ball to the side with his first touch. But it wasn't perfect. Dmitri closed him down, and the two met shoulder to shoulder. Dmitri was tall but very skinny. He stuck out a leg, reaching the ball first, but Riley's shoulder charge knocked him off the ball.

"Foul!" Dmitri cried as he stumbled backwards and fell, his spiky blond hair resembling the quills of a porcupine.

"Play on," Samantha said. "Fair charge. But good press!"

Dmitri waved a hand in disgust but didn't complain out loud. Coach Anderson eyed Riley with approval.

Riley sent the ball to our left fullback, who tried to pass up the line. But Marco, the Colombian right winger, snuck back to steal the ball. He made one long touch down the sideline and took off. His movements were very precise, ruthless even, and it made me remember what Emile had said about him.

A straight cold assassin.

Brock was forced to leave the middle and close Marco down. I thought Marco might try to take Brock one v one, but instead he chose to cross to the center, where Dmitri was waiting. Riley was there, too, and they both rose in the air, again dueling for the ball. Riley gave Dmitri another hard shoulder, but Dmitri was taller and reached the cross first, snapping a header to the right side of the goal.

JoJo dove and knocked the ball away, but Marco had raced inside, beating Brock to the rebound by half a step. Before JoJo could recover, Marco blasted a line drive into the side netting.

The newbies had tied the score with a goal very similar to ours.

As the half went on, I noticed a few things. First off, the

other team's defenders took part in the buildup a lot more than our defenders. Both Duncan and Kenji were very skilled with the ball, more so than Brock, our two fullbacks, and even Riley. Emile was especially good. He often came inside, acting like a central midfielder. He always looked composed and almost never lost the ball. But his defense wasn't as strong as the others—which is kinda important for a defender—and he liked to ball hog and showboat, which seemed to frustrate Samantha.

Both Ian and JoJo were amazing goalies. To be honest, I couldn't tell who was better. JoJo was as quick as a mongoose, but Ian was bigger and made better passes.

Up front, the newbies could really play. Dmitri ran like an angry cheetah, a blur down the center, and Marco was impressive on the wing. He wasn't flashy but played smart and always seemed to make the right decision.

In midfield, a war was in progress. Otto was winning the battle on his side, but in the middle, Goran and I fought hard for every loose ball. He played super rough. Every time we collided, my teeth rattled and a shiver went through my body. It was like playing against a brick wall with legs. Remember Krek, the bruising central midfielder from Prague F.C.? Well, Goran was just as big, and had better skills.

As the half wound down, we made a run down the sideline. Ajay ended up with the ball near midfield. During the play, he and Patrick had switched sides, so Duncan was defending. Ajay tried to kick the ball ahead and race past the Scottish fullback. This is pretty much Ajay's only move but he's very good at it.

The ball rolled and rolled and rolled, ending up near the

corner flag. Ajay won the footrace and reached the ball first, but Duncan, knowing he was beat, launched into a slide tackle that seemed to go on forever, and caught Ajay as he cut inside.

There was a scramble for the ball. It popped loose by the sideline. Somehow Duncan reached it first, shielded Ajay, took one dribble, and pounded the ball upfield.

The kick came down near me and Goran. We struggled to get position, and Goran won that battle. He backed into me, keeping me off the ball, and trapped the long pass. I reached around with a leg and poked the ball away. We both ran to it. Goran threw his hips into mine and knocked me off again. I thought it was a foul, but no whistle blew. Before I could recover, Goran was dribbling downfield.

I raced to get back, but the ball had already gone to Marco on the wing. This time, instead of racing for the corner, Marco sent a back heel towards the middle, where Goran was running. It was a sweet pass that fooled our defense, and I was too far back to intercept it. Goran reached the ball just outside the penalty box and lowered his thick body for a one-touch shot.

Bam!

The powerful kick flew by Brock, who tried to stop it with a leg, and sailed into the top left corner, just past JoJo's hand. It was a killer shot. Feeling guilty I had lost Goran, I jogged back and congratulated him on the goal. His only response was a grunt.

⚽   ⚽   ⚽

Soon after, the halftime whistle blew. My team jogged to the sidelines and gulped down water, ashamed we were losing 2–1 to the newbies.

Brock stood with a hand on his hips, still catching his breath. "C'mon, Knights. We can't let these guys beat us."

"They're not coming down the middle," Riley said. "I promise you that."

Patrick pointed two fingers at the sky. "Luckabucka, let's wreck 'em."

"That big kid in the middle?" JoJo said, and I guessed she was talking about Goran. "I don't like his face. Leo, take him down."

"Easy," Samantha said. "These are your teammates."

Brock crossed his arms. "Not today they're not."

"I'll do better this half," Ajay said, fiddling with a white sweatband on his wrist. "I'll get more crosses in."

"Duncan's tough," Samantha replied. "You're faster but you need to release the ball quicker. Don't give him time to catch up."

"Yes, Coach."

"I'm not going to say too much right now," Samantha said. "You're playing fine, but I can tell you're all a little rusty. We just want to get a sense of what everyone brings to the table, so play hard but don't hurt each other. I will say that you're letting Emile sneak inside too much. Otto, drop back more on defense, so they're not overloading Leo in the middle."

She looked my way. Her eyes lingered on mine, and I thought she might offer some advice. Instead, she clapped her hands, wished us luck, and walked over to discuss the first half with Coach Anderson and the newbies.

⚽ ⚽ ⚽

When the second half began, I was still tired, wondering where I would find the energy to finish the game.

But I had to push through.

The newbies started off strong, working the ball down Marco's side. He crossed to the middle. Brock headed the ball away, but it fell into the lap of their left winger. He took a hard shot that JoJo saved and slung out to Otto.

My big Hungarian friend turned and led Patrick down the wing. Screaming like a banshee, red hair flying, Patrick ran straight at Duncan, beat him down the sideline, then sent a ball on the ground to the middle. A defender slid to intercept but missed. I let the pass roll through my legs, fooling a second defender, and our right mid took a shot from the edge of the box.

Ian dove and caught the ball, jumped to his feet, and punted it downfield.

Back and forth it went. Both goalies made some excellent saves. Neither team could get a real advantage. As the morning sun got brighter and sweat dripped down my face, I received a pass and started to run forward, right at Goran. Wary of my moves, he scooted back, so I pushed the ball to the side and chipped a pass to Ajay on the wing.

My aim was just right. Ajay blew past Emile, who had crept forward, hoping to intercept a pass on the ground.

Ajay took the ball on the run and crossed to the middle. His aim was off, and the ball curved back towards midfield, where Otto just happened to be in the right place at the right time. With his first touch, he pushed the ball forward, then took a big step and slammed a shot on goal. The ball deflected off Kenji's leg and skipped into the back of the net, tying the game.

Kenji put his hands against his head.

"It wasn't your fault," Samantha said. "Shake it off."

By now almost everyone on our team was huffing and puffing. Only Riley, who never seemed to tire, looked fresh.

On the other side, Kenji appeared to be in excellent shape. After the ball caromed off his leg for the goal, he seemed even more energetic than before. Soon after, when Patrick finally got the better of Duncan, sprinting past him on the wing, Kenji raced over and slammed into him, taking out the ball, Patrick, and even himself. The two players ended up sprawled on the ground, but Kenji sprang up and helped Patrick to his feet.

Otto took the free kick. It bounced off the defense and fell to Emile. He used a slick move to spin around an opponent, then pushed off his chest with an arm. Still no whistle.

Emile headed upfield as the newbies took off for the counterattack. We scrambled to get back. This time, instead of keeping the ball too long, Emile sent a long pass over the defense, deep into our half.

Dmitri, Brock, and Riley surged for the ball. It was going to be a footrace. Brock was quickly left behind, and Dmitri, who was already running in the right direction, got a step on Riley. I think Emile's sweet pass had taken Riley by surprise.

Caught a step behind the tall Russian striker, Riley pumped his arms and sprinted forward, his rattail swaying behind him. At the end, knowing he was beat, Riley tried to grab Dmitri's jersey. But the striker held him off. It was a great run, and Dmitri finished it with a slick shot into the bottom right corner.

JoJo pounded her glove on the ground.

The newbies were up 3–2.

As Dmitri ran past Riley, holding a finger in the air, Riley gave him a little shove, almost causing him to trip. Dmitri sprang around to confront him, but Coach Anderson blew the whistle and settled both teams down.

It didn't stay calm for long. As Samantha called out, "Ten minutes!" both teams pushed as hard as they could. The game got ragged and almost funny because everyone was so out of shape. Mistakes were made, easy passes missed. Both teams shoved a lot and tried wild slide tackles. A permanent frown appeared on Coach Anderson's face, and he was forced to call more fouls.

Our team worked the ball around midfield, looking for an opening. I passed to Otto and surged forward, calling for a wall pass. Otto gave it to me. When I looked up, I saw Goran closing me down. I almost turned and passed back to Brock, but I hadn't tested Goran one v one and decided it was time.

I hesitated, letting Goran get closer, then turned and started to pass to Brock. Except I didn't follow through. As Goran came stomping in like a buffalo, I swung my body to the side, pulling the ball with the bottom of my foot, then pushed it past him. Goran's eyes widened, and he tried to bulldoze me, but I slithered through. Now I had some space.

My wingers streaked forward, and our striker drew one of the center backs. The other one, Kenji, was the closest defender to me. I couldn't delay because I knew Goran was coming after me hard. I kept pressing forward, and again faked a pass, this time to Patrick. Kenji knew I favored that side and cheated into the passing lane. But I stutter-stepped and pushed the ball forward, gaining a step.

Now I was right inside the penalty box, and I didn't hesitate. I whipped my right leg through the ball and smacked it in the sweet spot. The ball curved and dipped into the top of the netting, just beneath the crossbar. Ian missed the save by inches.

Tie game!

No time to celebrate. Our team hustled back into position. I really didn't want to lose to these guys.

The newbies tried to go through the center again. From the look on Goran's face, he was furious I had embarrassed him with that move.

Dmitri got the ball, but Brock closed him down. He stole the ball, passed to me, and roared, "Go, Yank!"

I knew Brock didn't want a tie game either. After I turned, I surveyed the field, sure that time was about to run out. Goran was nowhere in sight. Although I had room to dribble, I decided to try for a long ball down the right wing, where Ajay could outrun his defender. I drew my leg back to kick—and felt someone slam into me from the side so hard I fell to the ground, crumpling like a paper bag.

ENTRY #5

Showdown in the Sahara

A whistle blew, long and hard. As I groaned and pushed to my knees, I saw Goran standing over me with a satisfied look. He offered me a hand. I didn't reach for it because I was still too rattled to move. As his hairy mitt hung in the air, a huge body flew into him, taking him down just as hard or even harder than Goran had tackled me.

It was Brock. Now Goran was lying on the ground as my English friend stood over him, fists balled, daring him to get up.

Players from both teams swarmed us, shoving and yelling. Both coaches blew their whistles over and over.

As I struggled to my feet, wondering if we were about to have a team brawl on the second day of practice, Samantha and Coach Anderson flew into the middle of us.

"That's *enough*," Samantha said sharply. Her angry tone and Coach Anderson's looming presence brought everyone to their senses. Both teams calmed down, and Brock backed slowly away from Goran, staring him down and not offering to help him up.

"This game is *over*," Samantha said. "But practice is not. We're all going to shake hands and apologize to each other, then run Carolinas until we drop. After that, we'll eat lunch in the cafeteria like a family. Now line up, and I better not hear a single negative word."

By the time I walked off the field, still aching from Goran's rough foul, I was so tired I could barely stand. My leg muscles quivered like jelly, and blisters had started to form on the soles of my feet.

During lunch, the cafeteria was quiet except for the clang of dishes and Riley's noisy chewing. At the end of the meal, Samantha gave a stern talk about team unity. We had a light practice in the afternoon, and she made us switch partners with every drill.

The rest of the week went smoothly. There were no more shoving matches or angry words. But everyone was on edge. The competition for starting positions would be fierce. I hoped that, once Samantha picked the first team, everyone would get along better.

On Friday night, she announced we were going out for pizza in Lewisham. The place she chose was a high-tech entertainment center with video games, a bowling alley, and a dance floor. I suspected she wanted us to have fun and bond.

As we jumped out of the team bus and piled into the entertainment center, everyone was in a good mood, more relaxed than we had been all week. I walked inside with my arms around Brock's and Otto's shoulders, laughing as Patrick made fun of Ajay behind his back. Ajay was listening to music through his earbuds and bobbing his head like a chicken. Patrick stood right behind him and mimicked him. Those two were close friends, though I knew Patrick missed having Sami around.

It was interesting to see the clothes everyone had chosen

off the field. Sometimes the way people dress can tell you a lot about them. Not everyone. I never give much thought to my own outfit. Though maybe that says something, too.

It was still summer, so tonight I'd chosen a pair of shorts, the Messi T-shirt I had bought at the Barcelona stadium tour, and my Puma slides. Most of my friends were wearing something similar, supporting their favorite club. Brock wore Liverpool shorts and a tank top, Riley was wearing a Manchester United cap backwards, Otto had on a Bayern Munich jersey, and JoJo was slouched in a navy blue Millwall hoodie that looked a hundred years old. Patrick's outfit was as hilarious as always: a pair of white-and-black Juventus socks pulled to his knees, a polka dot headband, and a bright orange Naruto shirt.

A few players wore clothing from their national team. Ajay had an England jersey, Ian was wearing a South African World Cup hat, and Marco had on a yellow-and-blue Colombia T-shirt.

Duncan had his Rangers FC shirt tucked into his shorts. He tucked in his shirts on and off the field, wherever he went. The rest of us found this habit very funny, because it made him look even more like a little boy, but Duncan didn't seem to care when we roasted him. I respected him for that.

Dmitri and Goran walked inside at the same time, talking in a language I guessed was Russian or Serbian. They were best friends and always together. Goran had on cargo pants and a tight black T-shirt that clung to his muscular chest. Dmitri's blond hair was spiked even higher than usual, and a thin gold chain rested atop his white designer T-shirt.

The only person dressed fancier than Dmitri was Emile,

who strolled into the entertainment center in casual white shoes with no socks, black pants that narrowed at the ankles, and a shiny blue shirt with a popped collar. He was talking on his Apple watch in French, which made him seem very sophisticated. Since his mother was a diplomat, I imagined Emile had all kinds of important friends all over the world.

While Dmitri's and Emile's clothes looked expensive, Kenji took the prize for most fashionable. On the field, he was all business and rarely showed his personality. He played like a samurai warrior riding into battle. But tonight, he had left the Caravan in a blue leather jacket, glasses, ripped jeans covered in patches, and a white V-neck shirt with a purple star in the center. It seemed too hot outside for that jacket, but I didn't know anything about fashion, and Kenji obviously did.

After Samantha placed the order, we all mingled and played video games. Everyone was friendly to each other, but as the night went on, groups had formed, and it became obvious that some of the newbies weren't interested in talking to the rest of us. Goran was the leader of his group, Dmitri was his right-hand man, and Ian was always with them. Marco hung with them, too, though he didn't say much and didn't play video games. He always had a serious expression and seemed to be thinking about something important. Probably soccer.

Emile was also part of their circle. Every now and then, he would say something that made Goran and Dmitri and Ian burst out laughing. Marco might crack a thin smile, but I never saw him laugh.

Once the pizza came, Coach Anderson sat at a table with the newbies, while Samantha joined me and the other returning starters. Duncan and Kenji looked unsure where to sit, and a little lonely, so I invited them over.

"Kenji from Japan," Patrick said as we all grabbed pizza slices like they were about to disappear. "What are you, a fashion model or something?"

Kenji looked confused by the question, then ran a hand over the collar of his leather jacket. "I am not, Patrick from Ireland. This is very normal clothing in Japan. Boring, even."

"What?" I lifted my palms in the air. "If you're boring, what does that make the rest of us?"

Kenji looked solemnly around the table. "Very very boring."

We all chuckled, and Otto wiped a spot of tomato sauce off his mouth. "Where did you play before here? Tokyo?"

"Yes. At an academy similar to this one, but much less, ah, important. In Japan, we dream of playing in the English Premier League."

"So do we," I said. "In the United States."

"Do you like anime?" Ajay asked. "Or is that, you know, cliché in Japan, since that's where it started?"

"Oh, I like anime very much. Especially Jujutsu Kaisen and Naruto."

I high-fived Kenji, and Patrick smacked his chest atop the Naruto logo on his shirt.

Kenji continued, "I also like the Beastie Boys, Michael Jordan, Fruity Pebbles, and Taylor Swift."

The rest of us exchanged glances, unsure if he was roasting us.

Then we burst out laughing, confused by his random pop culture choices.

Brock put his meaty forearms on the table, leaned forward, and snarled. "What about fish and chips?"

"Most excellent," Kenji said.

"Liverpool?"

"The best forwards in the Prem."

As Riley groaned and smacked his forehead, Brock stood up, reached across the table, and thumped Kenji on the shoulder. "Good bloke!"

JoJo rolled her eyes. "Don't listen to 'em, Kenji. Not all Brits love fish and chips and football."

Riley and Brock turned towards her with disbelieving expressions. "Wut?" Riley said, throwing his hands in the air. "Course they do."

"I can't stand fish of any kind, and most chips are fat and soggy."

Riley spluttered. "That's just mingin' stupid."

JoJo put a palm in his face, then turned to talk to Samantha.

⚽ ⚽ ⚽

The pizza was delicious. After plowing through it, we wandered back to the video game area, which had neon strobe lights and a multicolored floor that lit up when you walked on it.

Towards the end of the night, most of my friends had gathered around a zombie shooter, but a racing game caught my eye. As I slid into one of the cockpit chairs in front of the screen, someone took the other chair, ready to challenge me to a race.

I looked over. It was Goran.

We locked gazes. "Would you like to race?" he said.

I put two tokens in the machine. "You're on."

He put in another two tokens. We chose our avatars and a race in the Sahara Desert. Goran opted for a green monster truck, and I chose a black sports car that resembled the Batmobile.

Engines revved.

The flag went down.

Goran and I shot forward, eyes on the screen, hands wrapped around the gear shifts.

No way was I losing to this guy in a video game.

Nothing compares to my love for FIFA, but racing games are one of my specialties. I guided my car expertly through a maze-like oasis filled with palm trees, tunnels of sand dunes as tall as skyscrapers, and underground caverns beneath the desert. I was destroying the computer-controlled cars and pulling away from the competition. Soon I was in first place, flooring the throttle and soaring high on my jumps to collect coins and special weapons.

But a challenger appeared, and I realized it was Goran. Despite all my efforts to shake him, he drew closer and closer. I had to admit, the guy could drive.

I unloaded hot oil, laser beams, and grenades into his path. Nothing slowed him down. As the final lap approached, we were neck and neck, and Goran even took the lead. I grimaced and went faster, forgetting about trying to wreck him and concentrating on speed instead. I pulled even again. I could hear him breathing beside me, grunting with the effort.

The finish line was just ahead. Both of our vehicles screamed across the ribbon of pavement slicing through the sand.

The checkered flag went down, signaling the end of the race. Fireworks burst in the sky, and special points were awarded. My hand tensed on the gear shift, and I leaned forward, waiting to see who had won.

"First place!" I said in triumph, as the number appeared above my car.

But Goran shouted the same thing, at the same time, and I realized another message was flashing at the bottom of my screen.

TIE GAME

What?

No clear winner?

What kind of video game was this?

Goran looked over at me. "Good race," he said grudgingly.

"You, too," I muttered.

"I guess we still don't know who's the best."

I had a suspicion he wasn't talking about video games.

"Should we race again?" he said.

Before I could respond, Samantha appeared beside me. "Time to go, guys. The bus is waiting."

After she walked off, I was still looking Goran in the eye. "Anytime," I said.

⚽ ⚽ ⚽

School started on Monday.

Now I had to wake up early every morning for conditioning with the team, attend class until two, and practice until dinner. Sometimes we had evening film sessions, and sometimes we had another light practice under the lights or in the indoor facility. The days were long and every night I collapsed in my bed, exhausted.

But I'd been here before. I put moleskin on my blisters, got plenty of rest and fluids, and soon I was fit again and ready to start the season.

We still didn't know who the starting eleven would be. Up top, Patrick didn't have any real competition, and Dmitri was a shoo-in for striker. On the right wing, I was worried about Ajay, because Marco was really good.

In midfield, no one had challenged Otto on the left, but we didn't have a natural right midfielder. Although Goran and I could both play the position, we both wanted to start in the center.

I guess we'd see who Samantha chose.

Emile seemed like a natural fit at left fullback. Duncan was probably the best choice on the right. At center back, Kenji was pushing Brock and Riley hard. All three were fierce warriors, and they each had their strengths and weaknesses. Brock was the strongest, Riley was the fastest, and Kenji had the best ball control.

In the goal, JoJo had a real fight on her hands to keep her starting position. Ian was coming on strong, and he was definitely Coach Anderson's favorite. I had a sneaking suspicion Coach Anderson had a few other favorites as well—like Goran and Dmitri—but Samantha was the head coach and had the final choice.

We wouldn't have to wait much longer. Our first game was just over a week away, and on Friday afternoon after practice, Samantha announced a team meeting for later that night.

After dinner, we would find out who the starters were.

ENTRY #6

The Starting Eleven

After practice, on the walk back to my building, someone picked me up from behind, pinning my arms to my sides. For a moment, I panicked, thinking Goran or Ian wanted to start some trouble. Or maybe Brock was just goofing around. But then I heard a familiar voice call out.

"Leo, bruv!"

John set me down, and when I turned, we did some special hand slaps and danced in a little circle. Though we'd chatted online, John and I hadn't caught up in person since returning from summer break. That seems hard to believe, but the U16s lived and practiced on the other side of the Caravan, and we'd both been so busy with school and soccer we just hadn't had time.

Like me, John was dripping with sweat, and his uniform was covered in grass stains. He was wearing slides and had his kit bag slung over his shoulder. Though shorter than I was, he seemed to have grown since the last time I'd seen him. Or maybe I was being paranoid about everyone's size.

"How's it, Leo? Good action out there? The newbies any good?"

"Yeah. They can play. We still don't know who the starters are."

"I heard Aron moved to the Dragons. That's a tough loss. But I also hear a dude named Goran is smoking up the field."

Even the U16s are talking about him? "Uh, yeah, I guess."

"Eh? Is his rep overblown?"

"He plays my position."

"Ah." John's broad face broke into a smile. "Then he'll have to find a new one, innit? Cuz you'ze a starter, bruv."

"I hope so. What about you? I guess you're a newbie, too."

"Hey hey, that's right. But I won't start this year. Not unless our striker gets injured. He's the leading scorer from last year and will get a schollie for sure."

"I'm betting on you anyway," I said, and shook my head. "Too bad we couldn't keep the same team this year. We'll never know if we could have won the title together."

"Not true, bruv. You'll be with us next year."

"I can't believe Caden got cut. Is your midfield that good?"

John seesawed his head. "Yeah, they're pretty bang-up. It was a close call though. And Caden landed on his feet. You heard he went to West Ham?"

"Really?"

"Yup. That's a solid academy. He'll be fine."

I said, "What about Eddy and Sami?"

"I dunno, why don't you ask them yourself?"

He was grinning and looking behind me. I turned and saw my two friends and former teammates walking through the grass. We all embraced and did another little dance. I noticed Sami's curly hair had grown a bit longer, while Eddy looked tanner and leaner. I remembered his parents lived in Miami and asked if he'd gone there for the summer.

"Yeah," he said. "I played lots of beach soccer."

Sami had taken a trip to Dubai because his family was rich and traveled all the time. John, like me, had stayed at home.

They had come all the way across campus to see me, and I walked them all the way back. We took our time and caught up with our lives. It was really good to see them, like part of my family had returned from a long trip. As we parted ways, they wished me luck in the first game, and I did the same.

"Hey, bruv!" John called out as I was walking away.

I turned. "Yeah?"

"Let's meet at the Cage sometime. And hit up Nando's after."

I wasn't sure when I'd have a free weekend, but that sounded great. "It's on."

They disappeared inside the U16 building, and I walked back to mine, wishing we were still on the same team.

Like John had said, I guess we could be one day.

If I made the U16s.

⚽ ⚽ ⚽

Later that evening, after dinner, we all moved to the lounge, where Samantha liked to make announcements. It was a large room, and we sprawled out on the chairs, bean bags, and leather sofas. My friends and I were sitting on one side of the room, and most of the newbies were on the other. I was squeezed between Brock and Otto on a short couch.

Samantha walked up to a whiteboard set up on an easel in front of the big screen TV. Our game schedule for the next few months was written on the whiteboard. Before Samantha started speaking, she glanced around the room and hesitated, making me wonder if she had noticed the separation among the players.

If so, she didn't comment.

She pointed at the top of the whiteboard, which read *Knights vs. Cavaliers*. After that, we had three more games before we played the Dragons at their home stadium.

"How many of you are eying the game against the Dragons?" Samantha asked.

That was exactly what I was doing. I, along with everyone else, let out a cheer, along with shouted promises to take down our archrival.

"That's a mistake," Samantha said quietly. "And a good way to lose the first four games." With an eraser, she removed all the games except the top one. "The Camden Town Cavaliers. That's the only team you need to focus on. You have to *earn* the right to fight for a title, and that happens game by game, play by play, practice by practice. Okay?"

"Got it, Coach," I said, and my teammates voiced their agreement.

She nodded in approval. "As you know, our first game is next Saturday. In a minute, we're going to discuss our game plan, and how the Cavaliers like to play. But first, I know you're eager to see the starting lineup."

As Samantha flipped over the whiteboard, the room grew silent, and everyone seemed to draw a collective breath. Absently, I reached down and rubbed my thumb against the front of the lion's tooth on my leather necklace.

On the other side of the whiteboard, Samantha had outlined a soccer field and written eleven names, position by position.

"4–3–3," Otto said. "Just like last year."

I noticed the same thing, but I was too busy searching for my position to worry about the formation.

Ah! There it was, the name of a player at the number ten spot, just behind the forwards.

And that name was mine.

"I'm starting," I said in a low, surprised voice.

Brock ribbed me in the side. "Course you are, Yank. Don't be mental."

He was starting, too, alongside Riley at center back. As I predicted, Emile was our left fullback, and Duncan was on the right. That left out Kenji. He was sitting in a chair beside Otto, and when I looked over, I saw Kenji's eyes lower in disappointment.

I leaned over Otto. "Don't worry," I said to Kenji. "You'll get plenty of PT."

When Kenji looked up, I saw a flicker of hope in his eyes. "I hope so."

Otto had kept his starting position at left mid. To my surprise, since Goran had played center mid in every scrimmage on the team opposite mine, he was starting on the right. I suppose the coaches thought he should be starting somewhere in midfield, no matter the position.

I glanced over and caught Goran glowering at me. A knowing little smirk crept to his lips, as if to say, *You may be the number ten for now, but watch out.*

That wasn't cool. We were supposed to be teammates. I resisted the urge to return the smirk and decided to ignore him instead. I turned back to the whiteboard to see who was playing up top. As everyone expected, Patrick was starting on the left wing, and Dmitri was the striker.

But I was surprised to see Ajay as our starting right winger.

When I looked over to see how Marco was taking the news, I saw him staring straight ahead, as emotionless as a boulder. I never knew what that guy was thinking.

JoJo high-fived Patrick, since her name was listed in the goalie spot. Ian did not look pleased. He was sitting behind Goran, and he leaned forward and whispered something to him, then nudged his head towards JoJo and snickered.

I released a deep breath. All of my friends had kept their positions, and so had I. But I knew Samantha preferred to make newbies earn their spot. So that might have played a part. Eventually, how we played in the games would be the deciding factor, and the season had just begun.

But for now, the future was bright, and we had some great new players in the starting eleven.

ENTRY #7

Game Time

Next Saturday arrived, a rare sunny day in London. Just before noon, I walked onto the field with the other starters, shaking out my legs, bouncing to stay loose, ready to play against the Camden Cavaliers.

You know that juicy good feeling at the beginning of the season, right before kickoff of the first game, when you're standing on the grass and waiting for the ref to blow the whistle, full of anticipation and nerves and excitement all at the same time? There's nothing like it, no matter if you're playing in the Youth Prem or the local rec league.

Why is this moment so powerful? Because anything and everything could happen during the season. You could score fifty goals or none at all. Your team could win the championship or sink to last place. You could play so badly you don't make the team next year or play so well that scouts across the globe are recruiting you.

What would happen this season?

The ref blew the whistle.

Time to find out.

Dmitri was standing in the center circle with his foot on the ball. He kicked off to Patrick, who swung the ball around to me. Last year, we lost 5–0 to the Cavaliers early in the season. They love to counterattack and play long balls to their wings, and their defense is tough, too. Their top player was an Italian fullback named Enzo, and I saw him on their right side again, lining up against Patrick.

I passed to Otto, playing it safe and getting a feel for the ball. I had so much adrenaline I wanted to take off downfield and try to dribble their entire team.

Otto sent the ball up to Patrick again. This time, he made a run down the wing, but Enzo cut him off and stripped the ball. The Cavaliers kept possession for a while, then pushed through the middle. When I stepped up to guard the ball, the opposing center mid passed to his teammate. Goran met him with a lunging tackle and knocked the ball loose.

There was a wild scramble. I reached the ball first, spun around a defender, created some space with my next touch, and hit Ajay on the run. He took off towards the corner and whipped a pass into the middle, but it went too far and allowed the defense to recover.

Back and forth it went, neither team able to dominate the game. Last year, our first game against them started the same way. We held on for a while, but they had scored first, then kept piling on the goals.

Would this year be the same? Maybe there wouldn't be a title challenge at all, and we would be stuck in the bottom of the league again.

My fears almost came to life when the Cavaliers drove deep into the heart of our defense, attacking on Emile's side. He clashed with their winger, but the Cavalier attacker won the battle and came up with the ball. Emile scrambled to catch him, but the winger sent a dangerous cross into the middle.

Their tall striker rose up high in the air . . . reaching, reaching . . . but Brock got there first and headed the ball away.

Riley ran it down. He made a slick one-touch pass to Duncan, who carried the ball upfield, his thick pale legs pumping beneath him. A defender approached. Duncan led Ajay down the wing. Ajay started to dribble and thought better of it, shielding a defender until Goran arrived to help.

"Go!" Goran roared, waving his hands to push everyone forward.

But I was already on the move. He saw me cutting and fed me in the middle. So far, his desire to have my position hadn't affected his play. At least not that I could tell.

A defender ran at me hard. When the ball arrived, I stepped over it, fooling him as I used the outside of my foot to cut back in the other direction. Another Cavalier stepped up. I sliced the ball around him and hit Patrick with a high pass.

"Kee-yaii!" he yelled, soaring high and snapping his neck for a header. The powerful shot clanged off the crossbar and back into play. Dmitri slid for the follow-up but just missed.

A Cavalier recovered the rebound and passed to a midfielder, who immediately kicked the ball long and hard, trying for a quick counterattack. Last year, in the first game, this team smoked our defenders time and again with their speedy runs.

But they hadn't been playing against Riley.

As their striker raced for the ball, Riley caught him from behind with an incredible burst of speed. He lunged, stuck out a foot, and touched the ball to JoJo, who launched a kick upfield.

The ball hung in the air. A bunch of players, me included,

gathered underneath it, fighting for position. As the ball came down, Goran plowed into us and knocked everyone out of the way—me included—to win the ball. I jumped up and raced forward, ready to help, but Goran kicked the ball ahead, a beautiful pass that split two defenders and rolled towards the penalty box.

Dmitri burst forward, racing for the ball. I was stunned by his pace. He was really, really fast. Within moments, he had outrun the defenders, and now it was a race against the goalie, who was sprinting to cut him off.

I held my breath.

Who would get there first?

It was super close, but at the end of the play, Dmitri slid and poked the ball forward, just around the keeper and into the goal.

1–0!

Whew.

We had started the season with a lead—but now we had to keep it.

And it wouldn't be easy. As the half wore on, the Cavaliers pressed us hard. They had a better midfield than last year, and forwards almost as fast as ours. With the half winding down, they earned a corner kick and sent a cross screaming into the box. Their striker reared back for a full volley, but JoJo leaped out of nowhere and snatched the ball, landing hard on her side.

The halftime whistle blew.

On the walk to the dressing room, I wiped sweat off my brow, wishing it wasn't quite so hot. The weather felt more like Ohio than London.

After Samantha congratulated us for playing well and gave us some advice, Coach Anderson stepped forward. He had a habit of crossing his arms and toeing the floor as he spoke.

"Not bad, Knights. Not bad. I know you're still learning how to play together, but I like what I see, for the most part. On the counter, try to close them down more quickly. Stop the ball before it continues. If you're outnumbered, don't stab at the ball. Back up and do your best to hold the line. Give your teammates time to support you. Goran, good toughness out there, and nice pass to Dmitri. Keep it up. Let's all give Dmitri more balls. Emile, tighten up that dribble, but good possession work. Duncan, I'd love to see a little more thought in your passes. Patrick and Otto, keep linking up. Oh, and JoJo—great save at the end."

He spoke a while longer but never said a word about me. I tried to shrug it off but wondered if I'd done something wrong. It wasn't the best half of my life, but I thought I'd played pretty well.

⚽ ⚽ ⚽

The second half started fine. We had a few near misses—Otto hit the crossbar, and Goran had a shot from way out that the goalie barely saved. On defense, we managed to stop most of their counterattacks in midfield. The one time they had a breakaway, Riley chased down their striker again.

1–0 is not a comfortable lead. Another goal would let me relax. The next time I got the ball, I wove upfield, evading a defender and then hitting a sharp ball to Ajay on the wing. It was a good pass, but Ajay had trouble controlling it. The defender recovered the ball and made a quick pass to his midfielder, who sent a line drive pass all the way across the field.

Emile stepped in and intercepted the ball. A smart play, but then he tried a fancy move instead of making the easy pass to Otto. His opponent stripped him and shot towards the goal with no one in his way.

Brock raced over to cover. He cut off the attacker's angle for a shot, but the Cavalier forward made a beautiful curving pass that hit their striker on the run. Because Emile had turned the ball over so quickly, Riley was out of position. The attacker took one dribble and lasered a ball into the bottom right corner.

1–1.

Instead of relaxing, now I was worried we would end up with a tie or even a loss.

"Emile!" Samantha yelled. "That's too much!"

He held up a hand. "Sorry, Coach."

Coach Anderson crossed his arms and frowned. Play restarted. The Cavaliers pressed harder than ever, keeping us on our heels. They smelled blood and were looking for the win.

A loose pass rolled through midfield. I raced for the ball and stutter-stepped as I approached, causing the defender to hesitate. Then I touched the ball forward and left him in the dust.

That opened up some space. I noticed Ajay making a run and chipped the ball over the defender, leading Ajay deep into the corner. He trapped the ball and turned, but the defender stuck out a leg and blocked his cross. Ajay tried to pass back to Goran, but the pass was too soft, and a Cavalier intercepted it.

Goran threw up his hands. "C'mon!"

Ajay looked deflated but I had to sprint back and defend. Duncan stopped the attack this time and played a nice ball to Otto.

I glanced at the game clock. Fifteen minutes to go.

JoJo made a save and threw the ball to Emile. A defender pressed him, and Emile tried to dribble around him. I cringed, waiting for him to lose the ball again, but this time he used a slick stepover to create space up the sideline. Then he made a crisp pass to Otto that started a counterattack of our own.

I raced forward. Otto saw me and didn't hesitate. He weighted his pass perfectly so I could run on to it. Open grass ahead. I took a long dribble to the right, saw Ajay open again, and hesitated. He hadn't played well this game, and they were probably leaving him open on purpose.

A defender was running straight at me. Time to decide.

I faked a pass to Ajay, slipping the ball to my left at the last moment. The defender stuck out a leg, barely missing the ball, and I slid past him, so close our jerseys touched.

Dmitri was frantically waving a hand, hoping I would feed him through the middle. It was a good option—but I saw a better one.

On my left, I noticed the fullback on Patrick's side creeping too far forward. The fullback was probably preparing to chase after Dmitri if he made another run. I glanced at my red-headed friend, and we locked eyes for a split second from across the field. I think he'd been waiting for that, because as soon as he saw me looking, Patrick took off, sneaking behind his defender. Patrick was moving fast, and it was a risky run. If I didn't pass the ball at once, he would be offside.

So I didn't wait. As another defender thundered towards

me, I shifted my hips and launched a pass over the defense, a hard curving ball with one target in mind. As the ball screamed in, Patrick launched into the air, whipped his torso forward like a snapping rubber band, and smacked the ball with his forehead.

It was no contest. The keeper was caught flat-footed as Patrick's powerful header screamed into the top left corner of the net.

ENTRY #8

A FIFA Rematch

With a cry of triumph, Patrick slid on his knees across the grass and fired arrows at the sky. We all ran over and mobbed him.

For the last ten minutes, Samantha put in some subs, including Kenji for Brock, and Marco for Ajay. The substitutions took some time off the clock and gave the newbies a chance to show what they could do.

Kenji's debut almost started in disaster. He and Riley ran an offside trap, but Kenji pushed too high, and the Cavalier striker almost scored on a breakaway. This time, not even Riley could catch him, and the striker streaked towards our goal with no one in his way.

No one except JoJo, that is. She raced out of the goal, and when the striker tried to dribble around her, she dove on the ball and smothered the shot.

"Well done, JoJo!" Samantha shouted. "Great work!"

Before long, Marco got his chance as well. I trapped the ball in midfield and was pressured hard by two defenders. To buy time, I did some fancy footwork and shielded the ball, spinning right and left and back again. Otto ran over to help, and I managed to slip a pass to him between the defenders.

Otto chipped the ball to Patrick, who made a slick one-touch volley to Dmitri. After chesting the ball to the ground,

Dmitri gave it back to Patrick. This time, Patrick crossed to Marco, who took one dribble forward, just past a defender, and took a hard low shot on goal. Marco had not wasted any time or movement. He had received the ball, taken a single clean touch, and whipped the ball at the keeper. The shot wasn't perfect, but a defender stuck out a leg, trying to intercept it, and the ball skipped over the keeper's hands and into the goal, giving us a 3–1 lead.

Before the game ended, Marco had another shot on target, and his clever runs opened up space for Dmitri and Patrick.

Oh boy. If Ajay wanted to keep his position, he had his work cut out for him.

I did, too, I thought as the final whistle blew. Goran had played an excellent game, though his style was much different from mine. Like Caden, Goran was an excellent passer but not much of a dribbler. He did not try to take people one v one. Unlike Caden, or me for that matter, Goran was a monster on the field. He ran hard, tackled harder, and intimidated players with his size and strength. He was an incredible shielder and almost never lost the ball. He had a great shot as well.

All in all, he played like a machine with chest hair.

"Nice game," I told him as we walked off the field.

Goran grunted, tipped his head in my direction, then walked over to Dmitri and slung an arm around his shoulder.

Someone chucked me on the arm. "Yo, great playing!" Patrick said.

"Thanks," I said slowly, my eyes still lingering on Goran and Dmitri. "You were awesome. Sweet goal."

"Yeah, cuz your pass was unbelievable."

As we approached the bench, Samantha was slapping

everyone's hand and bouncing with energy. We formed a line to shake hands with the Cavaliers, then celebrated all the way to the dressing room.

⚽ ⚽ ⚽

Later that afternoon, after a long hot shower, I headed to the lounge to hang out with my friends before dinner. Since I was the first one there, I decided to play FIFA against the computer, which isn't much of a challenge. I chose an old Barcelona team and played against Real Madrid. By halftime, I was winning 5–0. Boring. I started trying to score with Messi all by himself.

"Say, Boss, you need a little competition?"

At the sound of the familiar voice, I dropped the controller and leaped to my feet. "Tig!"

I hadn't seen my older friend since my return to London. His mohawk was higher than before, and he was dressed in white jeans and a purple T-shirt with a pair of sunglasses dangling from the neck.

He flashed a wide smile and fist bumped me. "What's new? Hey—that's a dope necklace. What kind of tooth is that?"

"It's a young lion," I said, then told him about the street performer in Paris who gave it to me.

Tig took a closer look, gave an impressed nod, and flopped his lean body on the couch. "So, are you ready for a rematch? I'm taking Samantha out for dinner, but I've got a few minutes."

I shrugged. "If you don't mind losing again."

"Don't think so, Boss. I've been practicing. I'm ready for you this time."

I yawned. "Whatever."

"We can play an *El Clásico*, if you think the new Barca can hang with Madrid. Or do you need Messi to win?"

During the professional season, whenever Barcelona and Real Madrid play each other in La Liga, the game is called *El Clásico*. An instant classic.

I grabbed the controller and selected the teams. "I'll take you down with Raphinha and Lewandowski, no problem."

"If I had Bellingham, it wouldn't even be a game. But I'm still gonna mop the floor with you."

Over the next few minutes, Tig and I roasted each other hard as we played. We jumped up and down and shouted after every goal, our eyes lasered to the screen. The score was tied 2–2 at halftime. Tig struck first in the second half, using Modrić to assist Vini Jr. down the wing. I roared back with a long-range strike from Sergio Busquets.

The clock wound down. We went back and forth, taking shot after shot. Each of us scored another goal. In the last minute, I used a sombrero flick by Raphinha that caught Tig by surprise. Then Raphinha hit the crossbar with a shot, and, before the defense could recover, Lewandowski raced in and poked home the winner.

Tig set down the controller with a sigh. "I just don't know how you do it. *No one* beats me at FIFA. Do you play with Barca all the time?"

"Barely at all, since Messi left."

He shook his head. "I'm taking you down one day."

"Good luck with that."

He walked over to the fridge and grabbed a can of sparkling water. "Want one?"

"Sure."

He tossed it over. "Nice win today. On the real field, I mean."

"Thanks."

He winked. "Think you're gonna challenge the Dragons for the title?"

"I don't know. I hope so. Have you played yet?"

"First game is tomorrow. I'm psyched."

"Hey, one of your managers met me at the airport. He said you're the starting right winger."

"Yeah. It's a big chance for me."

"He also said you had a bright future as long as you chose soccer over being a world-famous DJ."

"Ha! I'll save the DJing for my retirement. Who was that anyway? Bald Irish guy? Short and funny?"

"Yup."

Tig chuckled. "Danny's always giving me grief."

"Do you think . . . do you think you could get a call-up to the Prem this year?"

Tig leaned back against the couch. "Ah, Boss, I hope. It's possible, I guess. Probably not this year." He rapped his knuckles on a wooden table. "I don't even like talking about it. If it happens, it happens. Anyway, you should come see a game sometime."

"I'd like that."

"Lemme know, we'll get you right behind the bench." After a few minutes, he stood to leave and flung a hand towards the FIFA screen on the TV. "Ridiculous."

⚽ ⚽ ⚽

Over the next three games, we managed two wins and a tie. So far, Patrick and Dmitri were tied for the most goals at three apiece. Goran and I had two goals each and were tied for the most assists.

Our starting lineup had not changed. Samantha was still beginning the game with Ajay on the right wing, but she was substituting Marco at halftime. I was trying to stay positive about Ajay. He was faster than Marco and had a wicked cross, but Ajay didn't have a single goal or assist yet. That's tough as an attacker.

I think Samantha hoped Ajay would continue to develop, and that's why she kept starting him. But I had to admit he was a weak spot right now.

On defense, Kenji was playing amazing, but so were the starters. I could tell Kenji was frustrated, but he was helping our team by subbing for one of the other defenders when they got tired. In the goal, Ian continued to play well in practice, and I wondered if he would get a chance to start.

All in all, the season was going great. Only the Dragons and Liverpool had a better record than us. But it was early, and we had not played one of the top teams yet. That would change on Saturday, because our next game was against the London Dragons.

We were about to find out just how good we were.

ENTRY #9

Knights versus Dragons: First Joust

The next week, in addition to our long practices, we had end-of-quarter tests at school. It was hard to concentrate since I kept thinking about the game with the Dragons, but I forced myself to study and do as well as I could.

On Friday night, the team went on another outing. Samantha must have thought the trip to the entertainment center was good for team bonding. Or maybe she wanted us to relax before the big game.

This time, we took a bus to Greenwich, a borough on the banks of the Thames River. London has thirty-two boroughs, which are like small cities within London that manage their own parks and schools and things like that.

The bus ride took twenty minutes. After walking around Greenwich Village, an interesting part of the city with cobblestone streets and markets and lots of delicious-smelling food, Samantha took us to a large park with a monument to the Prime Meridian. I don't usually care about statues and monuments, but the Prime Meridian is kinda interesting.

What *is* the Prime Meridian, you might ask?

Good question. I didn't know either.

How to describe it? Well, you know how I'm always talking about the time change between Ohio and London? Especially when I'm trying to get in touch with Carlos? The difference is five hours, though sometimes, during daylight savings, it can be four hours.

The farther you travel, the more of a time difference you have. Paris is six hours ahead of Ohio, Greece is seven hours ahead, China is *thirteen* hours ahead, and, if you can believe this, there's a sixteen-hour difference between Australia and Ohio. By the time we wake up in the United States, their day is almost over!

I never thought about why all those time differences exist or how they're calculated. I still don't know all the details, but basically, a hundred years or so ago, some people got together and decided the world needed a home base, kind of, for time and distance. They chose this very place where I'm standing—a long stainless-steel line running between the cobblestones in Greenwich Village—to be ground zero, at least when it comes to calculating longitude and latitude for maps, and time differences for clocks.

So that's why Greenwich is the basis for all the other time zones. Ohio and New York City are in the Eastern Standard Time Zone and are five hours *behind* Greenwich, and all the places in the opposite direction, like France and China and Australia, are always an hour or more *ahead*.

So, in one sense, I was standing at the center of the world. Kind of cool.

After walking through the park, we strolled along the water and toured a huge old sailing ship, the *Cutty Sark*, that's a permanent exhibit in Greenwich. At one time, it was the fastest ship in the world. It's survived wars, terrible storms, and a fire. You can walk right onto it and explore the different levels.

After that, we ended the night at a fish and chips restaurant, which made Brock happy. The two of us were sitting at a long table by a window with Otto, JoJo, and Patrick. Outside, we had a view of the *Cutty Sark* and the city lights gleaming off the Thames.

"Mmmm," Brock said as he stuffed a giant piece of fish in his mouth. Then he poured vinegar on his chips—French fries, that is—and dug into those.

I squeezed ketchup on my plate and wrinkled my nose. "That vinegar smells awful."

"That's because you Yanks don't have any culture," Brock said between mouthfuls. "Vinegar is delicious."

"Mingin' right," Riley added.

"My mom used to soak my clothes in vinegar," I said. "That seems like a better use."

Brock snarled, waved me off with a big paw, and kept gulping down food.

After a while, our conversation turned to the game with our bitter rivals tomorrow. One way or the other, we all knew it could be a turning point in our season.

"The Dragons are 4–0," I said. "Top of the table."

Patrick was using his fingers like chopsticks to pick up French fries. "They've scored fourteen goals in four games. That's a lot, *amigos*."

"So far," Otto said, "they have the best offense in the league. Diego and Aron are tied for the most goals, with five apiece."

"They've got a new fullback who's really good, too," Brock said. "He's Brazilian like José. My dad says he's tops in the league. The fullback, not José. Well, maybe both."

Emile was passing by our table on the way back from the restroom. "Top fullback in the league? We'll see about that."

He kept walking and took a seat at the table he was sharing with Goran, Dmitri, Ian, and Marco.

"That bloke is too cocky," Brock muttered.

"Truth," Patrick said. "Let's hope he can back it up."

I watched Emile say something to the other guys at his table. I couldn't hear what it was, but they all laughed, glanced at our group, then looked away when they caught my eye.

Everyone, that is, except Goran, who winked at me before slowly turning around.

That guy was getting on my last nerve.

My gaze swung to a smaller table next to ours, where Ajay was sitting with Duncan and Kenji. As Duncan leaned over his fish and chips with a serious expression, like the meal was a test or something, Ajay started talking to Kenji and wriggling his fingers in the air, as Ajay often did. Every now and then, Kenji would manage a short reply, but Ajay kept talking over him. I realized Kenji was barely following his words.

"Listen," JoJo was saying. "My goal is gonna be like a bank vault tomorrow. Nothing gets in." She looked at Brock and Riley, her two chief warriors on defense. "Right?"

Riley pounded a hand into his fist. "They're not even getting *close*."

"I hope they do once or twice," Brock said with an evil grin. "So I can hammer some people."

"Just get the ball to Leo and Otto," Patrick said. "They'll get it to me, and I'll hand deliver it to the Dragons' goal."

Brock belched and thumped the table. "We crushed them

at the end of last season, and we're gonna do it again tomorrow."

The boasting kept up for a while. I laughed along with my friends but didn't add any comments of my own. Even though I knew they were just letting off steam, I preferred to talk on the field. To be honest, it made me a little superstitious to brag about a win before it happened.

Yes, we had beaten the Dragons. Barely.

But at the beginning of last season, they humiliated us with an 8–0 defeat.

I hadn't forgotten that either.

Now both teams had new players, and this is a brand-new season. Whoever wins tomorrow isn't guaranteed to win the league. Far from it.

But it sure will make a statement.

⚽ ⚽ ⚽

The next morning, I opened my window to gray skies and a light drizzle. By the time we boarded the bus for Dragon Stadium—this was an away game—the rain had stopped but a thick cloud cover remained. When we took the field for warmups, the ground was moist but not soggy. It could have been worse, and I didn't mind these conditions. At least it wasn't too hot.

Samantha named the same eleven starters and gave me the captain's armband. When she did this, I saw a slight frown appear on Coach Anderson's face, though he smothered it when he saw me looking. I knew he thought Goran should be playing my position and probably be the captain, too.

As I jogged out with my teammates, pumping my knees

and waving my arms to stay loose, I eyed the packed stands. I knew they were full of people who wanted to see the Dragons get revenge on us for spoiling their perfect season.

In the past, all those people might have intimidated me. But after our victory last year, and our run in the Tournament of Champions, I had learned to block out the fans and focus on the game.

It didn't work all the time. The energy of the crowd was a powerful force, almost like an extra player on the field.

But I was getting better at it.

"Let's go, Knights!" Samantha shouted. "Start strong!"

As we lined up in our positions, I looked across the field, surveying our opponents. The Dragons played a 4–3–3 like us. Charlie was hulking in the goal, slapping his gloves together. Hans and Mateo, two of my fiercest rivals from the Dragons summer camp, were the starting center backs. Both were huge and incredibly good.

I recognized the right fullback from last year, but the left fullback, a tall player with short, curly dark hair, must be the Brazilian left back that Brock was talking about.

José and Fabio were in midfield, along with a blond-haired right mid from Denmark that I also remembered.

Up front, speedy Sebastian was lined up on the left wing, with Aron on the right. I glanced Aron's way, but he was stretching and didn't notice me.

Finally, standing tall and proud at the edge of the center circle was Diego, the star striker who Tig had once said was the best player his age in all of Mexico. Now many people thought he was the best striker in the U14 Prem.

My old friends Sergi, Miguel, Conor, and Dayo were on

the bench. After the summer academy camp, the Dragons had chosen Dayo over me. The rejection gave me an extra boost when I played them. Maybe that wasn't the right attitude, but oh well. Nobody's perfect.

The referee checked with the head coaches and the linesmen, then blew the whistle.

Game on!

We had the ball first. After Dmitri passed to Goran, we worked the ball around the midfield, and Goran tried a long pass down the wing. Ajay settled the ball just in time for Hans to level him with a shoulder charge, then kicked the ball upfield.

José trapped the ball and tried to advance it, but Goran, Otto, and I raced back to cut off his angles. José passed to Fabio instead, who was forced to play the ball back to Mateo.

Right from the start, I could tell our team had lots of positive energy. We had come to play.

José received the ball in midfield. I pressured him hard. He shielded me off with one arm, turned upfield, and made a slick pass to Sebastian.

I shouldn't have let him turn like that. But when he shielded me, he seemed stronger than last season. As the game went on, this became more noticeable. Despite having a thin frame, José rarely lost the ball. He was quick and smart and knew when to pass. But in the past, if you caught him, he wasn't that strong and could be moved off the ball.

That seemed to have changed.

Had he put on muscle in the offseason? Or started working out?

When a pass went to Diego, he fooled Brock by letting the

ball roll forward instead of trapping it. Then Diego ran past Brock and shot towards the goal. Riley tried a slide tackle and missed. As Diego reared back to shoot, JoJo came flying out of the goal, trying to cut off his angle. Diego noticed and chipped the ball over her sliding body when she dove. I held my breath as the ball soared towards the open goal.

Clang!

Diego's shot hit the crossbar and bounced away.

Sebastian, their Polish right winger, darted in for the ricochet. He was very speedy and beat everyone to the loose ball, but Duncan slid into him and knocked it away.

The ball was still in the penalty area. Aron sprinted over from the right wing, but Riley cleared the ball with a powerful kick that caused Aron to stumble and almost fall. After the play, Riley nudged him in the back and said, "Traitor," loud enough for everyone to hear. Aron ignored him and ran off.

The ball landed near Otto. He was trying to shield off the blond Danish right mid, whose name was Mikkel. When the ball hit the ground, Otto threw his big hips into Mikkel, knocking him back. Mikkel was very quick and tried to dart around him, but Otto held him off and passed to Patrick.

"Let's go!" I yelled, racing forward.

Patrick hit me on the run. I gathered the ball and saw Mateo closing in. I was moving fast and thought I could beat him. As he came in from the side, I stutter-stepped, causing him to hesitate, then kicked the ball forward. He said something in Spanish and grabbed at my jersey as I went past. I slapped his hand away and kept going.

Just before I took a shot, Hans slammed into me from the side so hard it felt like being hit with a cement truck. Where had he come from? As I hit the ground and got a face full of grass, Patrick raced towards the loose ball, forcing a defender to kick it across the goal line.

Hans was looming over me. "Better luck next time, Leo," he said in his German accent. "There won't be a repeat of the last game, *ja*?"

I ignored him, jumped to my feet, and jogged into the penalty box for a corner kick. Mateo stood right by me and kept his big body between me and the goal.

"Don't you have someone your own size to cover?" I said.

He wagged his finger. "Someone else will have to beat us today. Because it won't be you."

"We'll see," I said.

Patrick's cross sailed in. It was coming right towards me. I fought hard for position, but Mateo shoved me aside, leaped high, and headed it away just before Goran made contact. As Goran came down, he put an elbow in my chest and shoved, causing me to stumble. I don't think he did it on purpose—it was chaos in there—but it still annoyed me.

The Dragons Brazilian right fullback—his jersey read *Pedro*—recovered the ball. Otto tried to challenge him, but Pedro nutmegged him and darted forward, starting the counterattack.

Pedro passed to Mikkel, who had room to run. Since Patrick had taken the corner kick, and Otto had just gotten beat, the left side of the field was wide open. Mikkel dribbled all the way to Emile, who came in too fast, trying for a highlight reel slide tackle. He should have held the line and given the rest of us time to get back.

Once Emile hit the ground, Mikkel passed to Pedro who

sprinted down the line. Pedro was very quick and had excellent touch. His first dribble was a long one into open space. Brock was forced to race over and defend, leaving Riley to cover Diego.

Pedro whipped in a cross. I cringed, knowing Riley couldn't handle Diego in the air. But the ball sailed over both their heads. Aron was the target instead. He had switched sides during the play. Duncan tried hard, jumping high on his stubby legs, but Aron was too big and powerful. He rose above Duncan and slammed a powerful header into the back of the net.

JoJo smacked a hand against the goal post, furious.

1–0.

"Hey, Leo," Aron said as he ran by me after the goal, running a hand over his high flat top haircut. "We had a good run last summer. No hard feelings, I hope."

"No hard feelings," I mumbled, not feeling confident enough to throw any trash talk his way.

As the half went on, one thing became very clear.

The Dragons were even better than last year.

Maybe a lot better.

Aron and Diego were a deadly combination up front. Both were tall, strong, and highly skilled forwards with a nose for the goal. Not to mention Sebastian, who was faster than Duncan on the wing.

It wasn't just the forwards. The last time we played our archrivals, I felt like I was better than José. This time, I wasn't so sure. As I said, he seemed stronger and more athletic, which made him even more dangerous.

On defense, Hans and Mateo and Charlie might be the

best combo in the league. Now they had Pedro as well. Not only was he good at pushing forward, but so far, he was shutting Patrick down.

As Otto gave me a pass in midfield, I snarled and vowed to play better. Someone had to step up, and I was the team captain.

"Here!" Goran said, waving on my right.

I slipped him the ball and ran forward, slithering past José. Goran gave it right back and continued upfield. Fabio tried to cut me off, but I spun, dragged the ball with the bottom of my foot, and left him behind.

A few fans *oohed* and *aahed* at the move. Behind me, I heard Fabio muttering in frustration in Italian.

"Great move, Leo!" Samantha cried. "Go!"

Up ahead, Hans and Mateo were lurking on defense, waiting to shut me down.

But we had numbers, and I planned to use them.

It was time to turn this game around.

ENTRY #10

The Battle Continues

I dribbled forward, ten yards outside the box, deciding what to do.

On my left, Patrick was racing towards the corner. Dmitri called for the ball in the middle, and Ajay cut inside, giving me a short option.

Hans stepped up, staying low, ready to take me on. Even if I beat him, Mateo was lurking behind him. I eyed the goal and saw Charlie covering the angle of my shot.

I shifted left and chose Patrick. My pass skipped past Hans and into the lap of my red-headed winger. As he settled the ball, I curled inside, hovering a few yards behind Dmitri.

Patrick's cross came in. It was off target, too high for me or Dmitri or Ajay to attempt a good header. The ball was passing just behind me, with no one around to collect it. If I didn't do something, the possession would be wasted. So I did the only thing that came to mind with a ball that high.

I tried a bicycle kick.

Hans backed off me, not thinking there was any danger. As the ball soared overhead, I leaped high and scissored my legs in midair. I hadn't practiced bicycle kicks in a while, and it showed. My left foot connected with the ball, but my attempt was much too high and wide, soaring out of bounds over the goal line.

Some of the Dragons snickered as I ended up on my back, gasping for air. The hard landing had knocked the wind out of me.

A hand reached out to help me up. "Good effort, Leo."

The hand was attached to a red-and-gold Dragons uniform. It was José. I accepted his hand and jumped to my feet, embarrassed by my attempt. José was just being nice. It was *not* a good effort. It hadn't been anywhere close to the goal. I glanced at the sideline and saw Coach Anderson glaring at me.

Soon after, the halftime whistle blew.

In the dressing room, the mood was grim, but Samantha did her best to lift our spirits.

"Does anyone remember the score at halftime from our first game against the Dragons last year?" When no one responded, she said, "It was 4–0. So chin up. We beat them once and we can do it again. One-nil doesn't mean anything. We're going to go out there in the second half and tie the score before they know what hit them. One goal at a time, Knights. Let's go!"

A cheer broke out, and I felt a little better. My pride was still wounded from my failed bicycle kick, but I had to move past it and help the team.

Both coaches talked tactics for a few minutes, and Samantha made the same change to the lineup as the last few games: Marco for Ajay at right wing.

On our way out of the dressing room, Brock held out a fist and looked me in the eye. I closed my fingers and bumped his fist with mine.

We knew what had to be done.

⚽ ⚽ ⚽

It began to drizzle again as both teams lined up for the second half. I wiped my eyes and waited for the whistle. When it came, I shot forward, pressuring José right away. He skipped to the side and passed to Fabio. The tricky Italian midfielder faked a pass to Sebastian, then crossed to Aron instead, all the way across the field.

Aron and Emile danced, with neither gaining an advantage. Mikkel arrived to help, and Aron used him. Then Mikkel passed to Pedro, who was racing down the wing. The Brazilian fullback cut inside and took a long shot on goal that JoJo batted away.

Our turn.

JoJo rolled the ball to Emile, who faked Mikkel out of his socks with a Ronaldo chop, then switched the field with a long pass to Goran. The Serbian gave it to me, and I gave it right back. Goran took a few dribbles and took a shot even farther out than Pedro's.

Crack!

The powerful shot rattled the goal post and bounced away. Charlie looked relieved, and I was impressed by the near miss.

"Great hit!" Coach Anderson called out. "Let's see more of that!"

On our next push, I slipped a pass between Hans and Mateo, leading Dmitri on a breakaway. But his first touch was a little off and took him too far left. Before he could recover, Hans stole the ball.

Samantha clapped. "Well done, Leo."

Dmitri was having a rough day. He couldn't shake Hans

and Mateo. They either drew him offside or sandwiched him for a hard tackle. My pass had been Dmitri's only real chance to score all game.

Hans passed to José. I tried to intercept it but just missed. José skipped away from Otto and hit a hard diagonal pass to Aron, who came back to receive it. When he turned, Emile was there to challenge him. Aron stood with a foot on the ball, hesitating, then took off again, blowing by Emile.

That was too easy. Emile had to do better on defense. He chased after Aron, but the big Swiss winger thundered downfield and launched a line drive cross to Diego. Brock was right behind him, and I didn't think Diego could do much. Surely he would have to chest the ball and play it back?

But Diego surprised everyone by leaping and volleying the ball straight out of the air. It was an incredible shot that most players would not even have attempted. As the ball left Diego's foot, taking off like a guided missile, JoJo leaped to her left, matching Diego's amazing effort with one of her own, reacting so fast it stunned me. She managed to slap the shot away with a single outstretched hand.

But luck was not on her side, and the ball went right back to Diego. Since JoJo was still on the ground, he tapped it in for an easy score.

Sebastian laughed in our faces on his way back to his position. "This is too easy. I thought you guys would be tougher."

Brock shoved him in the back, causing Sebastian's gangly body to take a tumble. Diego rushed over to defend him and stuck a finger in Brock's face. Riley raced over to defend Brock, and Hans and Mateo jumped in. Before I knew it, half the players on both teams were shouting and shoving.

The whistle blew, over and over.

A yellow card whipped out for Brock, and another for Diego.

"Knights!" Samantha yelled. "Enough of that! Calm down and play the game!"

Both teams settled down, but from that point on, it was war. Every tackle was extra hard, and some of the shoulder charges sent players to the ground. Three more yellow cards came out, for Patrick and Hans and even Otto, who rarely lost his cool.

"You can't play with us, Leo," Fabio said as he ran by. "This league is ours."

"Is that why we beat you the last time?"

"That was last year. Different players, different teams. We own you now."

I knew he was just trying to rattle me. Fabio was notorious for playing dirty and trash talking. He wasn't even that good, just an average athlete with a nice touch who somehow always managed to be in the right place at the right time. I guess that *did* make him good, but I didn't like how he bent the rules and tried to get in other players' heads.

The next stretch of play was frustrating. We had to get back in the game but couldn't get the ball. It felt as if we had barely touched it this half. The score was only 2–0 but it seemed worse. We just couldn't get anything going. Every time we tried to hit Patrick in the air, or Dmitri on a breakaway, Hans and Mateo shut it down.

Otto was growing tired. Emile was sloppy with the ball. I was barely keeping up with José.

A loose ball bounced around in midfield. Fabio recovered

it. He tried to put a move on Goran, but the Serbian shouldered him off the ball. I had to admit, if anyone was holding their own today, it was Goran. He tackled so hard that our opponents almost seemed afraid of him.

When a defender stepped up, Goran darted forward and passed to me. José closed me down but didn't get too close, wary of my moves. I was forced to pass back to Emile, who pulled off a nifty one-touch chip over José's head. The ball landed right at my feet as I was curling around him. Every time Emile made a bad play, he made up for it with an amazing one.

I dribbled forward, eying my options. Mateo was stuck to Dmitri like a tight sweater. Patrick was waving his arms, but Pedro had dropped back to cover him.

I veered right and saw Marco cutting inside, drawing their left fullback. I wasn't sure what Marco had in mind because he was running towards me and away from the goal. Maybe he was just giving me an outlet.

Hans was sprinting right at me. I had to decide.

I took a gamble and passed to Marco. Once I released the pass, I ran towards him, calling for the ball. Marco gave it to me. Hans tried to stay with me but fell a step behind after my quick cut. I took another dribble and ended up just outside the penalty box.

Marco spun around his defender. I hit a pass with the outside of my left foot, curling it towards Marco, just out of reach of another defender.

It was a clever pass, but it left Marco facing the sideline instead of the goal. But when he received the ball, he rolled it backwards and evaded another defender, gaining an inch of space.

That inch was enough. Marco took one dribble towards the goal and rocketed a shot at the near post. Charlie was there waiting, but the shot was so close and hard it glanced off his hands and went into the net.

Stunned, I threw my hands in the air and ran over with my teammates to congratulate Marco. Unlike the rest of us, he barely reacted. His expression was cool, calm, and collected. Icy, even. Nothing rattled that guy. Not even a slick goal that put us back in the game.

"Let's push, Knights!" Samantha yelled. "We're only down one. Another goal and it's a new game!"

Being down one goal instead of two is a huge difference. Two goals feel like a mountain to climb. One goal feels like it could come at any moment.

I looked up at the clock. Fifteen minutes to go. We had to keep pushing.

Marco's goal gave us a boost of energy. We pressed hard and managed another shot on goal, a long-range blast from Duncan that Charlie swept up like a vacuum cleaner. Then he threw it halfway across the field—the only keeper our age who can do that—and the ball landed right at José's feet. I tried to catch him, but he was too far ahead.

Goran ran over and threw his body into José. Just before the collision, José toed the ball to Fabio. The ref started to call a foul on Goran but waved his arm instead, the signal to play the advantage.

Fabio crossed to Mikkel, who one-touched the ball to Sebastian. The Polish winger darted down the sideline, a step ahead of Duncan's lunging slide tackle. Everyone thought Duncan was finished for the play, but somehow, he jumped up in time to block Sebastian's cross. Stunned, Sebastian was forced to pass back to José.

Huffing and puffing, I challenged José for the ball, knowing he avoided one v one situations. But this time, José stuck an arm out, pushed me away, and took off. I thought the ref would call a foul, but he didn't. By the time I recovered, José had streaked ahead.

Riley ran forward to defend but he arrived too late. José smacked the ball right on his laces from just inside the box, a powerful shot that curved in towards the top right corner. I held my breath, feeling responsible for the missed tackle, hoping JoJo would make the save or the ball would sail out of bounds.

The ball whistled towards the goal with no spin, a dangerous knuckleball curling towards the corner.

JoJo dove and stretched out her body, her fingers reaching, reaching, reaching . . .

Splash.

The ball hit the back of the net.

I sank to the ground with my head in my hands.

As the Dragons celebrated, a strong arm lifted me up. "C'mon, Yank," Brock said. "This isn't over."

I nodded and rose to my feet, exhausted and bitterly disappointed in myself.

After that, we tried to get back in the game, but we couldn't even get the ball. The Dragons subbed in fresh legs, too—Miguel, Sergi, and Conor—making it even harder. In midfield, José and Fabio were running Otto and me ragged. Samantha was forced to take Otto off, and she probably should have yanked me, too. I just couldn't keep up with José.

With time winding down, I desperately wanted another goal. When I finally got the ball, I passed to Goran and looped around him, calling for it. But he had other ideas. He passed ahead to Marco, who sent a wicked cross into the box. Bodies went flying. Patrick dove for a header, forcing Charlie to punch the ball out of bounds.

Thirty seconds to go.

On the corner kick, Samantha sent everyone forward, even JoJo. Every goal mattered in the Prem, even last-second ones that would not change the result of the game but might count towards the goal differential in the table.

Patrick took the corner. It was a good kick, and I thought Brock had a chance to head it, but Charlie darted out of the goal, leaped high, and snatched it out of the air. In one smooth motion, he threw a long ball to Diego, who turned to race downfield.

Riley, Kenji, and JoJo sprinted to get back. But they had pushed too far forward, trying to flood the penalty box. When Diego received Charlie's throw at half field, there was no one between Diego and our goal.

It was still a long way off. If Diego tried to dribble all the way downfield, Riley would probably catch him. But that's not what Diego did. Instead, his right leg swung back, and he launched a powerful kick that soared across the entire half of the field. The ball bounced twice and rolled into an empty goal.

A dagger that pierced our hearts and signaled the end of the game.

ENTRY #11

A New Strategy

When the final whistle blew, I slumped to the ground, exhausted and disappointed, the cheers of the Dragons supporters ringing in my ears.

Our quest for the title had just taken a major blow.

In the handshake line, tempers were still high. José and I fist bumped and complimented each other, but some of my old friends, including Fabio and Sebastian, wouldn't look me in the eye. Diego never looked anyone in the eye, as if he was too good for this league, so nothing had changed there.

When Mateo passed by, a grin crept to his lips. "Better luck next time."

"Next time," I shot back, with confidence I didn't feel, "you're taking the L."

Charlie was in line after Mateo. "Don't think so," Charlie said. "I didn't even get a workout."

Brock was standing behind me. "We'll see you at the end of the season," he said.

"I'm looking forward to it. A sweep tastes good."

Ahead of me, I saw Aron approaching. Just before he got to me, Riley gave Aron a shove that knocked him out of line.

"That's what traitors get," Riley said.

Dayo was standing behind Aron. In retaliation, he gave Riley a shove, which led to more players shouting and pushing.

All the coaches ran over, calmed everyone down, and made us finish the handshake line. As soon as we did, Samantha told Riley to start running Carolinas. Still hot, Riley wheeled on Coach Samantha and started to say something. But when he saw the fire in Samantha's eyes, he turned and shuffled off towards the nearest corner flag.

In the dressing room, Brock flew to his feet and threw his water bottle down, which angered Samantha again.

"Sit *down*, Brock," she said. "Passion is good. I love that you care enough to be upset. But losing your temper is *not* good, and I won't tolerate it. That applies to all of you. I'll suspend you if it happens again."

Brock snarled. "They were chatting us up all game, Coach Sam. And some of their players wouldn't shake our hands. That's disrespectful."

"I agree," she said evenly. "Though some of you weren't angels either. I hope their coach addresses their poor behavior, as I will in practice next week. But do you remember the first game against them last year?" She crossed her arms and leveled her gaze at us. "None of that behavior was present. Why not? Because they didn't think of you as equals. Now *that's* a lack of respect. But at the end of last season, you rattled them. Ruined their perfect record. And they took it personally. They beat you today, and now they think they've got the upper hand again. And for now, they do." She paced back and forth, eying each of us in turn. "Do you know what the best form of revenge is? The only real way to make sure they don't disrespect you ever again? I'm talking about true disrespect, not a little trash talk and shoving."

"Win," I said.

Samantha turned to face me. "That's right."

Then she walked out of the room without another word.

⚽ ⚽ ⚽

Later that night, as I lay in bed trying to sleep, I relived the game in my mind.

It wasn't a pleasant experience.

Almost the entire game, I had felt outplayed, undersized, and overmatched. Our team didn't seem to have an answer for the Dragons front line of Diego, Aron, and Sebastian. And their defense, especially Hans and Mateo, had shut us down.

Charlie was right. Except for our lone goal, we had barely tested him.

And in the midfield, *my* midfield, I had to admit that José had gotten the better of me. I couldn't even be upset at him. I liked the guy and considered him a friend.

But I could be upset at myself.

The midfield was the engine of the team. Somehow, by the time we played the Dragons again, I had to figure out how to win the battle with José and give our team a chance to compete.

I just hoped we remained in the title hunt by then.

And that I was still our number ten.

⚽ ⚽ ⚽

The next morning, I woke to the sun shining through my window. I hopped out of bed, put on some good tunes at top volume, and sang along while I got dressed.

I don't believe in staying sad and depressed just because we lost. I mean, what's the point of that?

The day was young, it was still the weekend, and I had some pancakes to demolish.

On my way to the cafeteria, I noticed my leg muscles felt a little strange. Sure, I was sore from the hard game, but that was normal. It was kind of hard to explain, but my calves and thighs felt achy, almost as if my legs had the flu.

Weird.

I shrugged it off and assumed it was a different kind of soreness. By the time practice started on Monday, the strange ache had gone away, so I didn't think any more about it.

⚽ ⚽ ⚽

We won our next game 1–0 against the Shoreditch FC Archers. This was no great victory. Last year, the Archers finished in last place, and this year, they were only one spot higher in the table. Marco scored our only goal. He had started in place of Ajay, and I knew my friend would have a tough time winning his spot back.

Ajay just isn't a true winger. When I arrived at the Knights Academy, Ajay had started out as a midfielder. He was super fast but sloppy with the ball, so Coach Purcell had moved him to fullback. That didn't work either, but when Samantha became the coach, she tried Ajay on the right wing. I chuckled as I remembered what Samantha had asked me to do.

Don't make him work so much, she had said. *He can play the wing, I know he can, but he's thinking too much. Talk to him every time he touches the ball. Do the mental work for him.*

And Samantha's idea had worked. Ajay was really good at racing down the wing and crossing the ball. But those were his only true strengths. Marco was almost as fast as Ajay—not quite—and better at everything else. Dribbling, passing, defense. Marco was an excellent all-around player.

Would Ajay be stuck on the bench for the rest of the season?

⚽ ⚽ ⚽

The next week, my weird leg pains returned at practice. My heels and Achilles tendons hurt too.

I still wasn't worried. As far as I could tell, I wasn't injured, just in a little bit of pain.

But after the game on Saturday—a 2–2 tie against the Richmond Ravens—my feet and Achilles hurt so much that I limped off the field at the end of the game.

After the handshake line, Samantha walked over. "Are you okay, Leo?"

I grimaced. "Yeah. Just a little sore."

"No muscle twinges or anything? Do you need a few days to rest?"

Samantha had taught us the difference between playing through tired muscles—which is usually okay—and trying to play through an injury, which will only make it worse. So far, I didn't feel any sharp pain, or anything else that stopped me from running or kicking. Everything just hurt a little more, especially after the game.

Well, maybe a lot more.

"I'm fine," I said. "No big deal."

"Okay." She patted me on the shoulder. "Good playing out there."

I appreciated the compliment, but this was another disappointing result. There were sixteen teams in the U14 Prem. The Ravens were in ninth place, just below mid-table. This was a home game for us. If we were true contenders, we should have won.

One bright spot: The Dragons had tied Liverpool, so like us, they only received one point from the game.

As for my performance, I scored one of the goals against the Ravens and had an assist to Patrick.

Goran had the other goal, as well as an assist to Dmitri.

During the game, every time Goran scored or made an assist, he glanced my way with a little smirk. As if to say, *Everything you can do, I can do better.*

⚽ ⚽ ⚽

On Sunday morning after the Ravens game, Coach Anderson popped into breakfast to announce a special team meeting that would take place later that night in the dressing room beneath the main stadium. We often met there when we wanted to have a serious talk about strategy or tactics.

At seven p.m., my friends and I walked into the dressing room together. "What's this about?" JoJo said as we waited for the coaches and the rest of the players to arrive. "I got places to be."

Brock nudged JoJo's arm. "Like where? A tailor?"

She looked down at her ripped black jeans, then over at Brock's rumpled practice shorts. "Are you throwing shade on my style? You literally only wear footie clothes."

"Yeah? What of it?"

"If you ever want to talk to a girl, you might try something different."

The rest of us laughed, but Brock snorted. "Why would I want to do that?"

JoJo waved a hand in disgust.

"Samantha probably wants to discuss next week," Otto said. "We're playing Manchester, and they're fifth in the table."

"Probably right, Otto the Wise," Patrick said. "Talk about how we're gonna *sizzle* 'em."

Soon after, Coach Anderson walked in with Goran, Dmitri, Ian, and Emile. The five of them were laughing as if sharing a private joke.

Marco walked in next, followed by Samantha. I wondered if she had noticed how close Coach Anderson was to some of the newbies. I couldn't help thinking that he favored them over the rest of us.

"Hi, everyone," she said. "This meeting won't take long. I just wanted to introduce something we're going to emphasize going forward." She exchanged a glance with Coach Anderson, as if they had discussed this together.

I was curious now.

"As you know," Samantha continued, "we're not where we want to be this year. We're not doing badly. We're sixth in the table, which is far higher than this time last year. But who thinks we can do even better?"

Everyone did, and a thunderous cheer broke out.

"Me, too," she continued. "But we've had a few issues exposed, and something has to change if we want to compete for the title."

As I wondered what *issues* she had in mind, Samantha clasped her hands behind her back. "The Dragons have really improved their game this year. So have some of the other teams. As for us, although there are plenty of positives, both Coach Anderson and I think our lack of possession is hurting us. Even when we win, we don't always have the ball more than our opponents."

Uh-oh. Midfielders are the most important players involved in keeping possession of the ball and distributing it to the rest of the team.

Was Samantha about to make a change?

"I'm not making any changes to the lineup tonight," she said, as if reading my mind. "But going forward, we're going to work hard on keeping the ball more. This is one reason we brought in players like Emile and Goran, who are very skilled on the ball. Last year, we had a good run, but it wasn't built on possession." She turned to Emile. "Now, some of us aren't always perfect—"

"Guilty as charged," Emile said, which made everyone chuckle.

She smiled. "I like your honesty. I also like how you always attempt to keep the ball rather than kicking it away under pressure. Sometimes, you do too much, but that's okay. We'll work on it. That's what our practices this week will focus on: keeping possession."

I thought Samantha was overlooking Emile's poor defense, and I wondered how much Coach Anderson had influenced her decisions this year.

On the other hand, Samantha was the opposite of a pushover. I knew she would never agree to something she didn't want to do, especially as head coach.

So, if she said we needed to work on this, I trusted her.

For the next hour, Samantha stood at the large table with

the magnetic players and moved them around the model field, demonstrating some tactics we would use going forward. I enjoyed the lesson because I love to improve and learn about soccer.

But I couldn't help wondering what the new style of play would do to our team.

ENTRY #12

The World's Best Soccer Museum

The next weekend, we had a game in Manchester against the Marauders, the fifth-place team. Samantha decided to let us stay overnight so we could tour the city and the National Football Museum. I was excited about the trip. Last year, we had barely seen Manchester. Just popped in and out for the game. I think Samantha heard how much fun we had in Europe over the summer and decided to work in some sightseeing in England.

During practice that week, we focused on keeping possession. It wasn't that big of a change. We didn't switch formations or anything. But we worked a lot on moving the ball up from the back, all the way from JoJo to the forwards.

This was not JoJo's specialty. She did not have good foot skills. Although her throws and long kicks were improving, Ian was better at these. The big South African keeper was an excellent dribbler, too, which made it easy for our defenders to pass the ball back if they got in trouble.

JoJo tried hard in all the drills, but she kept losing possession. In a game, if a forward pressures her, JoJo kicks the ball long. But now, in that situation, the coaches wanted her to make a pass to a defender.

Time and again, when Patrick or Dmitri or Marco challenged her, JoJo tried to dribble to the side to create space for a pass. But her touch was poor, and our forwards kept stealing the ball, which set them up for an easy goal.

At one point, JoJo slammed a hand against the goal post. "I'm a keeper, not a dribbler. I save shots and punt 'em out."

Coach Anderson frowned, but Samantha raised her palms, calling for patience. "It's the first day," she said. "It takes time to learn these skills."

"I'm doin' my best," JoJo muttered.

"I know."

When it was Ian's turn, he had no problem evading our attackers' attempts to steal the ball. Ian would smoothly take a touch or two in one direction, then slip an easy pass to Duncan or Emile. Sometimes Ian would even step over the ball or dribble behind his legs.

Brock also had trouble with the new strategy. Riley used to be a forward, so he had decent foot skills, but Brock was a traditional English center back: big, tough, and good with headers and long kicks. He wasn't terrible at dribbling like JoJo. In fact, he was even better than the players on the fancy club teams back home. But still, this was the Youth Prem, and the standards were very high.

As for the rest of the defense, Duncan and Riley were decent at keeping possession, but Emile was on another level. When he moved inside with the ball, looking for a pass, it was like having another midfielder. His defense hadn't improved, but unless he was trying to be fancy, he almost never lost the ball.

I didn't have to change much. All three of our starting midfielders—Otto, Goran, and I—had excellent ball control.

Samantha had us work on helping the defense more and making sure everyone had someplace to pass the ball.

Up top, Samantha didn't want the forwards to change the way they played on offense. But if they lost the ball, she wanted them to press hard and fast to recover possession.

"The first few seconds after you lose the ball are the most important," she said. "That's when the other side is most vulnerable. Chase them down, pressure them, and make their life miserable."

⚽ ⚽ ⚽

Though October had just begun, the leaves were already changing color. The bus ride through the countryside on Saturday morning was beautiful, full of red and gold trees blowing in the wind, and we arrived in Manchester before noon.

Our bus pulled up to a hotel near a giant, cream-colored stone cathedral in the middle of the city. I stepped out of the bus and stretched my legs. It was chilly and windy. After dropping our bags, a guide took us on a walking tour through the Medieval Quarter, a scenic area near our hotel. We saw lots of colorful brick buildings, parks, and people sitting at cafés. The city was buzzing, and I liked it.

Oh, and soccer swag was everywhere. Man City this, Man United that. Jerseys, hoodies, posters, keychains, everything you might want to buy to support your team. As you can imagine, with great local clubs, the city was a bit nuts for soccer. I even saw graffiti and giant murals of players painted on the sides of buildings.

After the walking tour, Samantha took us to the National Football Museum, a modern glass building in a pretty park near the hotel. Though tall in the front, the museum slopes down to ground level at the rear. From the side, it resembles a giant glass soccer cleat. It's very impressive as you approach it. Imagine a whole museum dedicated to soccer!

Can you guess what was inside? I had some ideas, but I was blown away by how big the museum was.

At the entrance, we poured through a set of revolving doors, bought tickets, and walked onto the floor of the "pitch" level, which is built to look like a soccer field. There were photo exhibits on the turf floor, along with glass cases showcasing replica trophies from the Prem and the FA Cup. One of the trophies was real. You had to put gloves on to touch it.

An escalator led to the next level, called the Match Gallery. This was a huge floor full of historical items such as the earliest jerseys ever worn, the first rule book (from 1863), the first cleats, the first shin guards, the first stadium turnstile, and . . . you get the idea. They have all kinds of important trophies, historic game balls, clothing worn by famous players, basically anything you can think of that relates to soccer.

This level also had videos and interactive screens with information on most of the pro clubs in England. Things like clips from old matches, uniforms that teams have worn over the years, and league stats throughout history. I love stats, and that was a fun exhibit.

Next up was the Play Gallery. This was not a play area for little kids, as you might be thinking. It was much better: A place to test your soccer skills with interactive games that were a mix between real soccer and video games. We played four of them: On the Ball, Shot Stopper, Pass Master, and the Penalty Shootout.

Do you know what happens when you take a bunch of ultra-competitive academy players to a museum with a fun skills exhibit?

You get some serious competition.

We tried the Pass Master first. With this game, you have three tries to kick a ball against a wall painted with circles. You get points for hitting the circles. Kind of like Skee-Ball for soccer. The higher point targets were smaller and in the corners. Each player went twice, and Marco surprised everyone by scoring the most points, though he seemed bored by the game, and the museum in general. I didn't believe he was actually bored. That doesn't seem possible. Some people just like to pretend they're cool and bored all the time.

Goran and I were only a point behind him. Unlike Marco, Goran and I celebrated every high score, and so did the other players.

Otto and Patrick did really well, too. Of course, Patrick had to invent a new way to play the game by flicking the ball up and trying to use his head.

We played On the Ball next. With this game, a hologram player demonstrates a move or a trick, and you have to copy the skill on a pad with sensors that record your movements.

The moves and tricks were easy at first. Cruyff turns, scissor kicks, volleys, rabonas. But they got harder and harder: elasticos, around-the-worlds, rainbows, Okocha flicks, the roulette, and other advanced moves. Somehow, the game judged how fast and well you performed each skill.

I took home the gold medal. Not even Goran came close to my score. The next best was Emile, who I have to admit has some sick moves. After we finished, Emile congratulated me on my tricks, which seemed to annoy Goran.

Next up was the Shot Blocker. As you can imagine, this was meant for goalies. This game tests your reactions by sending holographic soccer balls towards the goal. You had to swat them away, and the balls came faster and faster. We all tried it; it was fun to play keeper for a day. I did pretty terrible, though Otto was the worst. I laughed so hard at his failed attempts that he actually got mad at me.

Want to guess who the best goalie was who wasn't actually a goalie?

Patrick did pretty well. So did Dmitri and Duncan.

But Riley killed it. He was *fast*. He scored so high that Samantha and Coach Anderson exchanged a look as if to say, *That might be our new backup goalie if someone gets hurt.*

The real competition, however, was between Ian and JoJo. Sometimes it's hard to judge who the best goalie is. They can't go one v one like other players. Sure, you can see who blocks the most shots in games and practice, but no two shots are alike.

But in this game they were, and there was a clear winner. JoJo.

Ian did well, but JoJo demolished his score. She knew Ian showed her up in practice last week, and she played the Shot Blocker game with a vengeance. After she won, she winked at Ian and spread her fingers as she walked away, as if doing a mic drop. The rest of us shouted her name and stumbled into each other, impressed by the dominant performance.

In the final game, we lined up against a virtual keeper in the Penalty Shootout. Every player took five shots at a digital goal made to look like Wembley Stadium, where the FA Cup final is played.

The game analyzed our power and precision. Brock took home the gold medal for the hardest shot. No surprise there. Goran was close behind him, and Patrick came in third, followed by me and Otto and Marco. Emile did not have a very powerful shot, but it was accurate, which he proved by coming in second on the precision test.

I tied for first on this skill, again with Goran.

"One more round," Goran boomed in his deep voice. "Leo and I need to know who the winner is."

I stepped forward, ready for the challenge. My friends gathered next to me, and Goran's group stood close to him.

"Sorry," Samantha said. "We're out of money, and it's time to go. We have dinner plans."

Goran grumbled as he walked away. I followed behind him, wondering who would come out on top in a true head-to-head challenge. I had a feeling that before the year was over, we would find out. Little did I know that day would come sooner than expected.

But first, we had a game to play against the Marauders.

ENTRY #13

Knights versus Marauders

The game started at noon on Sunday.

As the starters took the field, I bounced on my toes to stay loose, feeling good except for the ache in my legs that just wouldn't go away. Normally I didn't feel sore until after a game or a long practice, but today the pain was already there, jabbing at my feet and calves like an angry hornet. It worried me a little, but I pushed it aside and focused on the game.

Last year, the Marauders crushed us 6–0 near the beginning of the season. But we had gotten revenge after Samantha took over, beating them in the second game by one goal.

I saw a lot of the same faces, and they still had their best player, a tall and wiry French striker named Nuno. He had a lightning-quick first step and could leap like a startled cricket. Although both of their center backs were newbies, they were just as big and imposing as the defenders from last season.

So far, the Marauders were fifth in the table, one spot above us. It would be a tough game—and one we needed to win.

After the kickoff, when Patrick sent me the ball, I had an ugly flashback from our first game last year. I had passed the ball like a robot, afraid to upset Coach Purcell. Samantha had given me the freedom to play like I wanted, and I did just that, starting the game with a nifty touch to my right, slipping past a defender. I faked a pass to Goran, rolled the ball forward with the bottom of my foot, and hit Marco on the run.

Our Colombian winger ran down the ball but decided to pull back. He found Goran near the sideline. A Marauders midfielder charged forward, but Goran shielded him off with ease, turned, and switched the field with a long ball to Otto.

I took off, knowing Otto liked to play the ball into the space behind Patrick. And he did, leading me perfectly. I made a one-touch pass to Patrick and sprinted into the penalty box. Red hair flying, Patrick danced with his defender, broke loose, and raced towards the goal along the touchline. The goalie was forced to come out, and Patrick slipped a pass to me. I didn't have the best angle, so I stepped over the ball and kicked it behind my leg to Otto, who was running in behind me.

Otto's powerful foot struck the ball and rocketed it toward the goal.

Clang!

Just off the crossbar.

"Well done, Knights!" Samantha cried. "Way to start strong!"

As a defender collected the loose ball, I caught Samantha's eye, and she gave me a thumbs-up. I raced to get back, feeling good.

The Marauders pressed down the left wing. Goran narrowly missed an interception, leaving Duncan to defend. A Marauder forward tried to beat him down the sideline. He was fast but Duncan stayed with him, shoulder to shoulder. The winger cut inside with a slick stepover. I thought Duncan was beat, but let me tell you, that guy never gives up. He ran after the winger and caught him with a slide tackle just before he crossed the ball.

The Marauders had a throw in. The left midfielder looked around the field, then tossed the ball to Nuno. Riley was right there, fighting hard, but Nuno put a long leg forward, shielding Riley and searching for a pass.

He found his center mid streaking forward. The Marauder tried to put a move on Brock, faking a pass and then going for a nutmeg.

Brock didn't fall for it. With a grunt, he shouldered the attacker off the ball, then turned and passed to JoJo.

JoJo hesitated, knowing the coaches wanted her to keep possession. She tried to pass to Duncan, but Nuno anticipated the pass, and JoJo's hesitation allowed him to intercept it. As he darted forward, all alone with the goal, Duncan sprinted in from the side, flinging his body to the ground to try to block the shot.

It wasn't enough. Nuno was too quick, and he poked the ball into the net.

JoJo leaned over and smacked her palms on the ground, furious with herself. I saw Coach Anderson shake his head, while Samantha crossed her arms and pursed her lips.

Oh boy.

That was far too easy.

The whistle blew. We worked the ball around. A Marauder stripped the ball from Patrick, but Otto stole it back and made a quick pass to Emile. Instead of heading down the wing, Emile pushed the ball inside, fooling his defender with a Ronaldo chop.

He threw his hands forward. "Go!" he cried, then launched a quick ball over the top of the defense.

It was a clever pass that caught everyone off guard. At first, I thought Emile had kicked it too far, but Dmitri ran it down with a shocking burst of speed. The Marauders keeper, a burly player with freckles and lanky brown hair, raced out of the goal. Dmitri tried to lift the ball over him, but the goalie slapped it down.

The ball was loose in the penalty box. Marco arrived first, with a defender right on top of him. Marco flicked a pass to me with the outside of his foot. I was streaking forward on his left, but still behind him. How had he seen me?

Didn't matter. I had the ball in the penalty box. Both center backs lunged towards me, but I split those trees with a quick ground pass towards the left side of the goal. I wasn't sure if anyone would be there, but Patrick liked to make that run, so I gave it a shot.

The keeper scrambled to get back. The goal was wide open. I held my breath, not sure if anyone would reach my pass. Just when I thought it would roll out of bounds, Patrick gave a kamikaze yell, burst out of a pack of defenders, and dove with his right leg forward, the tip of his cleat reaching the ball just in time. It rolled into the back of the net, and I raced forward, jumping on him in celebration.

1–1!

A few plays later, the Marauders almost scored again. This time, when Nuno pressured JoJo, she managed to pass to Emile. But her aim was off, forcing Emile towards the corner flag. By the time he turned, the winger had him trapped. Or so I thought. Instead of kicking it long or trying to hit it off the defender, Emile lifted the ball over his opponent's legs, a neat flick that carried him to safety.

"Here!" I cried, racing back to support him.

Emile slipped me the ball. I heard a defender closing in. Using my hands, I felt his jersey, then spun with the ball and shielded him off as I turned upfield. As the defender grabbed at my arm, knowing he was beat, I whipped a pass ahead to Otto, who one-touched it to Patrick. As Samantha cheered and ran up the sideline, urging us on, Patrick surged deep into the corner. He fired a wicked cross into the box. The center backs closed in, but Marco rose high and snapped a header towards the top right corner. I thought it was in—right before the keeper dove and slapped it away.

It was an amazing save, and the last chance of the half for either team.

⚽ ⚽ ⚽

As I walked slowly to the locker room, breathing hard and sucking down water, my legs started to hurt. Knees, thighs, and especially my heels and Achilles tendons. Once the game started, I had forgotten the pain, but now, as the adrenaline wore off, it returned with a vengeance. I winced as I sat on the bench, causing Samantha to walk over.

"Leo, are you okay?"

"Yeah. Sure."

"Is something injured?"

"Just playing hard."

Her eyes lingered on mine. "Okay then."

I didn't want her to know I was hurting because I didn't want to sit out. I had to finish the game and help my team.

"Not bad," Samantha said, talking to everyone. "A few hiccups here and there, but I like what I'm seeing." She turned to Emile. "Listen, I know we're focused on possession, but there's a little too much dribbling going on." She clasped her hands behind her back as she paced. "Dmitri is pretty fast, isn't he? So are Patrick, Riley, Leo, and a lot of you. That Marauder striker is a real speedster, too. But what's the one thing on the field that moves far faster than even the quickest player?"

"A bird?" Patrick said helpfully.

Samantha rolled her eyes. "I said *on* the field."

"Sometimes birds land on the field."

"The ball," Dmitri said in his thick Russian accent. "Yes, it moves even faster than do I."

"I believe it does, Dmitri. I think you all get the point. Keep possession but move the ball. Dribble when you have to but pass if you can. All right, we're going to make a couple of changes for the second half. Ian, we're putting you in the goal. Kenji, you're in at right back. JoJo and Duncan, you're both playing well, but we want to see how this looks."

I glanced at my friends, feeling bad for them both. Duncan gave no sign of emotion other than to look Samantha in the eye and say, "Yes, Coach," in the same firm voice he always used.

JoJo hung her head and didn't say a word. After the halftime speech, before we all filed out, I saw Samantha sitting beside JoJo and talking to her. I couldn't hear what they were saying, but JoJo was nodding miserably, as if she agreed with Samantha but didn't like it one bit.

⚽ ⚽ ⚽

The Marauders started the second half with a strong drive that led to a powerful shot by Nuno. Ian knocked it aside. A good save, but I thought JoJo would have caught it. Anyway, Riley gathered the loose ball and made a risky pass back to Ian.

A winger sprinted in at top speed. Ian didn't have time to pick up the ball. I thought for sure he would clear it out of bounds, but instead he took a perfect touch to his left, just out of the winger's reach. This opened up space for a pass to Emile. Another Marauder closed in, but Emile whirled and fired a long pass to Goran.

He fed the ball to Marco. A center back tackled him and stole the ball. Soon after, Ian made another save. This time, he slung the ball almost to half field, putting the ball right at my feet. Impressive. I sent the ball to Dmitri, whose first touch got away from him, but wow. Ian's long throw had really started our counterattack.

As much as I wanted to see JoJo in the goal, I could see why the coaches wanted to give Ian a chance. If he wasn't such a jerk off the field, I might have been okay with it.

Though I still think JoJo is better.

So far, the second half was pretty even. I forgot about my leg pains and worked hard in midfield, making runs to support my teammates, driving the ball forward, and getting back on defense.

We pressed upfield. After Patrick lost the ball, he turned around and chased his defender down. Just before the defender kicked the ball away, Patrick stuck a foot in, blocking the kick. Our coaches cheered his effort, and when Otto recovered the ball, the defender looked stunned that Patrick had caught up to him. He had listened to Samantha and was good at going into kamikaze jet-pilot mode, as he called it, as soon as he lost the ball. Not everyone could do that, because it takes a lot of energy, but Patrick never seemed to tire during a game.

On defense, Brock and Riley had shut down the middle. I could tell Nuno was getting frustrated.

Emile was playing well this half, and so was Kenji. The Japanese warrior was a different kind of right back. Duncan had a great header and a killer cross. But Kenji had good ball control and was better at dribbling.

One thing they had in common: both were tough and never gave up. Though Duncan had a sturdier body, Kenji would run right into players and fling himself across the field for slide tackles.

Back to the game. Time was running out. Neither team wanted a tie. We all wanted to win three points and move up the table.

When Ian slung a long ball to Dmitri, I thought we had a breakaway, but one of their center backs flew in to make the stop. He kicked the ball upfield, and off they went in the other direction.

Nuno got the ball and pressed forward. As Brock stepped up, Nuno hesitated, then passed to his left. The winger took one long dribble and tried to outrun Kenji. At first I thought the winger had succeeded. He went past Kenji and raced down the sideline. But Kenji kept running. As the winger cut inside, Kenji let out a fierce cry, slide tackled him from behind, and knocked the ball loose.

Nuno sprinted to the ball and tried a slick turn around Riley. But Riley flattened him, knocking the ball loose again. No foul was called. Brock ran over and launched the ball upfield. He was supposed to be looking for short passes, but I don't think he cared. Sometimes, you just have to kick the ball.

The ball hovered high overhead and was headed my way. A midfielder pressed right against me. As the ball came down, I gave him a little bump with my shoulder to create space, then let the ball hit the top of my foot. I gave it a soft landing—which is really hard to do on a ball that high—then pushed it forward with my next touch, carrying me past the midfielder.

Open grass ahead. I dribbled until a defender stepped up, then led Goran on my right. He took the ball in stride and pressed forward like a bull. Another defender approached. On the wings, Patrick and Marco were calling for the ball. Dmitri was sprinting down the middle, waving an arm.

Goran was five yards outside the box. What would he do?

I was chasing him from behind, giving him another option. As I caught up with him, calling for a square pass, I thought Goran had waited too long. Another defender closed in, trapping him. But Goran held that defender off with a strong arm, took one touch, and surprised everyone by launching a shot on goal. He hit the ball square on his laces, and it took off like a cannon, a knuckleball shot that bobbed in midair, making it hard to control.

I held my breath as the powerful shot screamed towards the bottom right corner. The goalie dove, stretched and got his fingertips on the ball . . .

But it wasn't enough. The shot went in!

Goran bellowed and threw his arms in the air. We all rushed him, celebrating the goal. He even slapped my hand, though he didn't thank me for the sweet pass.

After that, the Marauders pressured us hard, but our defense stayed strong, and we held on for the win. Otto and I walked off the field with our arms around each other's shoulders, satisfied we had played a good game and controlled the midfield. If I'm being honest, I felt a little jealous that Goran had scored the winning goal. I'd never felt that way before. I was always happy when my team scored, no matter how it happened. That guy just seemed to bring out the worst in me, and I knew he wanted to take my position.

But I was thrilled we had won the game and would leapfrog the Marauders in the table.

As our team gathered on the sideline, I realized my legs hurt more than ever. With every step, it felt like someone was swinging a hammer at my calves and poking hot needles into my Achilles. After the handshake line, I could barely walk off the field, and it took all of my willpower not to let it show.

What was wrong with me?

ENTRY #14

The Two v Two Showdown

We had a light practice on Monday, and I suffered through two more days after that. Then I breathed a huge sigh of relief and collapsed on the field, because now we had a four-day weekend for fall break.

On Sunday, I called home and told my dad about my aching legs. He asked a lot of questions and seemed concerned, but he wasn't sure what was going on.

"Hey, kiddo, do you have a team doctor?"

"Yeah," I said slowly.

"What did they say?"

"I haven't . . . I haven't told anyone. It's not that serious. Just a little soreness."

"It sounds more serious than that." He was quiet for a moment, then said, "You don't want them to know, do you?"

I shuffled my feet. "No."

"*Leo*. That's not smart. You have to tell them."

"It's just strange, Dad. It doesn't feel like an injury. I mean, I'm already feeling better."

"Didn't you say you could barely walk after the last game?"

"Yeah, but—"

"That's not soreness, kiddo. Something's going on. Let them know, okay?"

"Okay."

"Promise?"
"Promise."
"Good."

⚽ ⚽ ⚽

After hanging up with my dad, I sat on the edge of my bed with my head in my hands. I *was* feeling better after three days of rest. In fact, my legs barely hurt. I bet everything was okay now. I wouldn't break my promise to my dad—I'd see the doctor if it happened again—but maybe a little break was all I needed.

I was lonely and ready to see my friends. Brock, JoJo, and Ajay lived in London and were home with their families for the break. Patrick had taken a train to Ireland, and Otto had flown to Budapest. I know that sounds far, but it's only a two-hour trip from London.

Of the returning players, only Riley and I stayed at the Caravan. I wasn't sure what was going on with him. I knew Samantha was still his guardian, or something like that, and he had a tough situation at home in Manchester. When we visited the city, he hadn't said a word about seeing his family, and no one ever came to watch him play.

Since the episode with Aron, Riley hadn't caused any trouble. At least not more than usual. Things seemed normal on the outside, but I felt that deep down, Riley was sad about something. I recognized the hollow look in his eyes because it was how I felt when I thought about my mom sometimes.

Except Riley's look almost never went away.

I tried to find him a few times over the break, but whenever I knocked on his door, he was gone. That or he didn't want to answer.

John had family plans, and Eddy was in Miami. Exploring London wasn't much fun on my own, so I stayed inside most of the time, resting my legs. I listened to a lot of music, chatted online with my friends, and played video games in the lounge. Tig stopped by once, and we had another FIFA battle. Actually we had ten battles. And he lost them all.

⚽ ⚽ ⚽

I finally saw Riley on Sunday night, at the end of fall break, when a bunch of us gathered in Brock's room to hang out. When I walked in, Patrick was standing on his head beneath a Man United poster, Otto was playing chess on his phone, Riley and Brock were arguing about who would win the Prem this year, and Ajay was sitting at Brock's desk with his glasses on, trying to study while Patrick pestered him to join him on the floor.

Ajay rolled his eyes. "Why would I want to do a headstand?"

"It's good for blood flow," Patrick said. "I'm meditating down here. Self-improvement. You should try it sometime. Trust me, you need it."

"You aren't meditating. You're talking. How is that self-improvement?"

"If you have to ask," Patrick said solemnly, "you'll never know."

"You're ridiculous."

"You're the one studying in a room full of your friends."

"I have a practice college entrance exam tomorrow."

Brock snorted. "We're in eighth grade."

Ajay mumbled something and closed his book.

"Do you have any music?" I asked Brock. He opened a laptop that looked about thirty years old—Brock wasn't a gamer—and pulled up a playlist on YouTube. I'd never heard any of the songs, and they were all pretty lame. I questioned his choice of music, and he got defensive.

"Hey, Yank, who made you the music police?"

"No one. I just have good taste."

"You play something, then."

I put on some tunes, and everyone except Brock immediately agreed that my music was much better.

I flopped on the bed, Otto finished his game, and we all roasted each other for a while. Brock opened a bag of chips he'd brought from home and passed them around. We were all in a great mood until we started talking about the team.

"I don't know about these changes," Brock said.

"I know about 'em," Riley chimed in. "They're rubbish."

Otto shrugged. "The best pro teams dominate the ball. I do think we need more possession."

I noticed Ajay was staying quiet and staring at the wall.

"I don't mind," Patrick said. "I'll go luckabucka bonkers no matter how we play."

Brock growled. "I just don't know why Samantha is messing with the team. We won the Tournament of Champions! What about you, Yank? What do you think?"

I hesitated. "I'm a center mid. I like to have the ball. But she can't bench JoJo. And we need Ajay's speed out there."

"You're being nice," Ajay said in a defeated tone. "Marco's a better winger than I am."

Patrick chucked him on the shoulder. "You need to be on the field. You're one of our fastest players, and definitely the smartest."

"I resent that remark," Otto said.

Patrick flung out a hand. "Whatever. You two can have a trivia duel or something."

We all chuckled and fell silent, before Otto said quietly, "The Dragons beat us pretty bad. If we want to win the league, we need to make some changes."

"Maybe," Brock said. "But it doesn't mean we need to change players."

We continued arguing about what needed to be done, but I stayed quiet, because I wasn't sure what the answer was.

⚽ ⚽ ⚽

The next day, Samantha had a surprise for us.

"Welcome back," she said as we gathered on the field after school. Earlier, Coach Anderson had led us through our morning conditioning. Now he was standing next to Samantha, holding a large clipboard.

"I hope everyone had a great break and got plenty of rest," she continued. "I thought we'd start the week with something a little different. Which of you likes swag?"

We all did, and we let her know it.

"I thought so. I happened to pick up a pair of official Knights tracksuits over the break. Maybe two of you would like to have them?"

"Yeah!" Brock said. "What size?"

"Whatever size you need. If you win the competition, and they don't fit, I'll exchange them."

"Competition?" I said. "What competition?"

Samantha put her foot on a ball. "The two v two tourney we're about to have instead of practice. A little welcome back present from me. After that, it's takeout pizza for dinner."

This time, we cheered even louder.

A two v two tourney? Bring it on!

"Do we pick our partners?" Brock asked, slinging an arm around my shoulder. "Cuz I've got the Yank. I need those trackies."

"Sorry," Samantha said. "I picked the teams myself. Coach Anderson, would you do the honors?"

"Sure." He looked down at the clipboard he was holding. "In no particular order, we have Ajay and Emile, Marco and Patrick, Goran and Otto, Riley and Kenji, Brock and Duncan, and Dmitri and Leo."

Dmitri and I exchanged a weak smile, neither of us too excited about the partnership. Coach Anderson continued reading out names until he had paired all the second-team players as well.

It was obvious what Samantha was doing. Every returning player had a newbie for a partner. She knew that ball possession wasn't the only thing our team needed to improve on.

We had a chemistry problem, too.

"Hey!" JoJo said. "Wut about the goalies?"

"Oh, you're playing, too. Every single game, in fact." Samantha pointed at the field, where I noticed two half-size goals set up about twenty yards apart, with cones for out of bounds.

JoJo slapped her gloves together. "Alright then. Good luck scoring on those pint-sized things."

Samantha outlined the rules: three goals to win, no offside, and no throw-ins or corner kicks; if the ball goes over the end line, the defense gets it.

Our coaches would ref the games. Samantha had even brought out a pair of large speakers and put on some music to make it seem like a party.

Because of the number of teams, the brackets weren't perfect, so most of us had a bye for the first round. That included me and Dmitri. In the second round, which had eight games, none of the teams with starters had to face off against each other.

But in the third round—the quarterfinals—things got interesting.

Dmitri and I were set to play Patrick and Marco. That would be a tough game. But first, Ajay and Emile would battle Brock and Duncan.

Samantha hadn't just stuck all the returning players with newbies. She had chosen a mix of styles. Brock and Duncan were physical players who put their noses down and bullied their way upfield. Ajay and Emile, two of the skinniest players on the team, relied on speed and quickness.

Had Samantha done this on purpose? Set up the brackets so that certain teams were likely to face off?

Probably. When it came to coaching, I knew she had a reason for everything.

Each game would start with a drop ball. As Coach Anderson stood in the center of the field, holding a ball with the Knights logo, the rest of us lined up on the sidelines, ready to cheer on great plays and roast every mistake.

Dmitri was standing right beside me. He was a few inches

taller, and his spiky blond hair added another inch or two of height. It felt like he was looming over me.

I think Dmitri considered himself very good-looking, because in the bus and the restroom—wherever there was a mirror or a window—he was always checking himself out and touching his hair. To me, he was just a bony guy with a narrow face. The sharp angles of his jaw and cheekbones jutted out in the same way his knees, elbows, and spiky hair did. It almost seemed like someone had cut him out of a piece of cardboard.

During the first two rounds, the two of us barely spoke off the field. "Who do you think will win?" I asked as the game started.

Dmitri watched Brock shoulder Ajay off the ball. "Probably the big two. They are too much, how do you say, muscle for the two little ones."

Little ones? I didn't consider either Ajay or Emile *little*. Emile was my size, and Ajay was the same height and build as Dmitri. "Size isn't everything," I said. "Emile is really good, and Ajay is the fastest player out there."

"That is true," he admitted, as if realizing my analysis applied to his own game. He shrugged. "We shall see, yes?"

I tried to talk to him a little more, but he didn't seem interested in conversation. I got the impression that Dmitri didn't like me very much and thought Goran should be starting at center mid.

Back to the game. It really was a clash of styles. Brock scored first when Emile tried to get too fancy in front of his own goal. Brock tackled him and blasted a shot right through Ian's hands. But Emile made up for it on the next play by whirling around Duncan and feeding Ajay a beautiful long pass that Ajay tapped into the goal.

No one scored for a while. Brock and Duncan played tough on defense. Whenever Ajay made a run down the wing and gained a step, his cross to Emile was always intercepted.

Finally, Emile threw up a hand. "Try something different!" he shouted at Ajay. "Be creative!"

His comment drew a hurt look from Ajay and a reprimand from Samantha. But on the next drive, Ajay did try something new. As Brock closed him down, Ajay faked a cross, cut inside, and blasted a left-footed shot that ricocheted off the goalpost. Emile stuck a foot in just before Duncan arrived and poked the ball past JoJo for a 2–1 lead.

Soon after, Brock and Duncan connected for a nice combo that allowed Duncan to break through on goal. Ian raced out to stop him, but Duncan pushed the ball to the side and curved a shot into the top right corner. I was impressed. I didn't know he could score like that.

"Next goal wins!" Coach Anderson said.

The rest of the match seemed to last forever. Emile danced around his larger opponents, dazzling everyone with his skill, but somehow Duncan or Brock always found a way to shut him down.

In the end, I think Brock grew a little tired. Even Duncan was sweating hard on the last play, when Emile made a nice through pass to Ajay, who outran everyone and flicked the ball past JoJo from five yards out.

Brock roared in dismay and fell on his back. Duncan stood with his hands on his hips, breathing hard and looking disappointed.

"I suppose you were right," Dmitri admitted. "The little ones won."

Ajay went to slap hands with Emile, but the Cameroonian fullback turned and ran to the sideline to bump fists with Goran and Marco instead. Had Emile just dissed Ajay?

"Great game, both teams!" Samantha called out. "Way to fight!"

Goran and Otto were up next. They had an easy game against two second-string players who couldn't match their size or skill. Goran and Otto made a fearsome team without any real weakness I could see. They won 3–0 within minutes.

Riley and Kenji also had a game against two subs. This game was even less competitive than the last one. Both Riley and Kenji are as fast as greyhounds and play hard all the time. Almost as soon as the game started, it was over 3–0, after two goals by Kenji and one by Riley.

"You're next," Riley said to Goran as he walked off the field, pointing a finger in his face.

Goran crossed his arms and stared him down. "I look forward to it."

I don't think this was what Samantha had in mind for team chemistry. But if Riley didn't like someone, he didn't try to hide it.

Their game would be a semifinal, and I wasn't sure who would win. But first, we had to find out who would play against Ajay and Emile in the other semifinal.

"Leo and Dmitri, Patrick and Marco," Coach Anderson said. "You're up!"

Patrick ran past me, clicking his tongue and flicking his wrists. "Luckabuckle up, Leo. The PM train is coming."

I grinned and said, "The train might be coming, but it's about to go off the rails."

Dmitri looked confused by the exchange and muttered something in Russian. Marco ignored our banter and jogged onto the field the way he always did: cool, calm, and collected.

I hunkered down for the drop ball, ready for a tough game. Patrick and Marco were both forwards and had a ton of offensive firepower.

But so did we.

"Ready?" I asked Dmitri. He nodded and touched his hair one last time.

Samantha dropped the ball between me and Marco. The Colombian winger's foot darted out, trying to win the tackle.

But I was faster. Before Marco could reach the ball, I flicked it to Dmitri. Then I took off and called for a pass.

I wanted Dmitri to lead me down the sideline. But as Patrick rushed in, Dmitri panicked and played the ball back to JoJo, our goalie for the game. She tried to kick a long ball to me, but Marco intercepted the pass and darted forward. I sprinted after him. Just before I caught him, he passed to Patrick, who burst away from Dmitri and slammed the ball into the goal.

"Choo-choo," Patrick said, pumping his arm up and down.

I ran back as JoJo was collecting the ball. "Nothing you could do about that."

"No," she said, looking right at Dmitri. "But someone can make better passes."

Dmitri sneered and waved a hand. "Just give me the ball and I will score."

I don't think it's quite that easy, I said to myself, then passed to him on the kickoff. We worked the ball around, looking for an opening. It's hard to get open in two v two. You have to move constantly and really use your partner. And one little mistake can lead to an easy goal for the other team.

Dmitri made another bad pass, and Patrick recovered the ball. He thought he had a breakaway, but I slid in from the side and tackled him. Dmitri outran Marco to the loose ball and kicked it downfield.

I raced after it. Ian rushed out of the goal to beat me to the ball. It wasn't the best decision. I got there first and nutmegged him for a goal.

1–1.

"Tricky-wicky, Leo," Patrick said. "But now it's on."

Patrick and I always roasted each other. We could be super competitive and never have hard feelings.

After the kickoff, Marco pressed forward with a grim expression, cutting one way and then the next. Dmitri dove in too hard for a tackle, allowing Marco to skip past him. Dmitri played defense like a snoring grandpa in a rocking chair.

Now they had a two v one against me. I feigned a step towards Marco, forcing him to pass to Patrick. I hounded him next, never getting too close, trying to give Dmitri time to recover.

Patrick passed to Marco, who gave it right back to his teammate. I scrambled to catch up. As Patrick started to shoot, Dmitri flew in and stole the ball, leaving Patrick kicking at air. At least Dmitri had raced back to help.

"Here!" I cried, knowing we had a chance for a quick goal.

This time, Dmitri listened. He passed to me and took off

running. Marco tried to cut me off, but I one-touched a pass right back to my speedy striker. Ian slid to grab the ball, but Dmitri took a touch to the side and slammed it home.

"One more to go," I said as Samantha gathered the ball.

Dmitri held up a thumb and crouched to defend.

They pressed us hard, trying to isolate Dmitri. Patrick beat him one on one, but JoJo flew out to stop the attack and won the ball. She threw the ball to me. I tried a long shot that Ian saved. Back to Marco it went. He darted forward, smooth as silk, and crossed to Patrick. I sprinted back. Patrick tried to beat me, but I stuck one leg behind the other, a nifty tackle that took him off guard. As we fought for the loose ball, Marco came out of nowhere and stole it.

"Get back!" I shouted to Dmitri.

Marco was heading straight towards JoJo. Dmitri arrived to help, sliding on the ground to steal the ball. But instead of panicking, Marco calmly drew the ball back and watched Dmitri sail across the grass. It was almost funny. Then Marco took two dribbles and slipped an easy goal into the side netting.

"Next goal wins," Samantha called out.

I wiped sweat from my eyes, took a few breaths, and kicked off to Dmitri. He started to make a run, then passed to JoJo instead. We worked the ball around but couldn't find an opening. For long minutes, neither team had a real chance.

After Patrick blasted a shot high and wide, I received the ball in the middle, with Marco coming on strong. We'd never really tested each other before. I knew he was a great all-around player, but how was his one v one defense?

Let's find out.

As he approached, I tried some feints, but he didn't fall for anything. Dmitri was calling for the ball and making a run. Patrick was guarding him tight. Marco got low, ready for anything.

I didn't think about what I did next. I practice a lot of moves, all the time, and sometimes they just come out of me. As Marco took a step closer, I flicked the ball into the air at knee height. Then I did an air elastico with my left foot. Except for doing the move in midair, this is just like a ground elastico: I swept the ball to the left and then forward, all in one motion, slipping the ball past Marco's left shoulder in midair. Then I took off in the same direction before he could recover.

Even I was surprised at how well that worked. An air elastico is a tough move, and Marco was caught flat-footed.

Patrick raced in to cut me off, but I touched the ball forward, just ahead of his slide tackle. Ian ran out, knowing he had to close me down, but I took another touch, just evading his leg. Then I passed the ball in for the winning goal.

"Oh no!" Ajay said, stumbling around the sideline as if he couldn't believe his eyes. "What a sick move!"

Even Samantha was smiling. "Good stuff, Leo."

As Dmitri and I shook hands with our opponents, Patrick gave me a playful shove. "Seriously? An air elastico?"

I shrugged and held up my palms.

As Marco walked off the field, Brock roasted him a little. "Like they say in the States, mate: Yank just posterized you."

Marco picked up his water bottle, took a long drink, and acted like nothing had happened.

Did anything rattle that guy?

"Very nice," Dmitri said gruffly to me, then turned and cheered for Goran as he ran onto the field with Otto.

The semifinals were about to begin.

ENTRY #15

Leo and the Giant

As I watched Otto and Goran kick off versus Riley and Kenji, my legs started to hurt.

I'm just a little sore from the first few games, I told myself, and proceeded to ignore the pain.

This was an exciting matchup. Riley and Kenji were electric to watch. Though neither had the ball control of Otto or Goran, the two slender defenders were so fast they could make up for their mistakes. Just when Goran received a pass from Otto and thought he had an easy first goal, Riley sprinted over, launched himself into the air, and blocked the shot.

On the other end, Kenji and Riley made runs down the middle, using their speed. Kenji, stylish as always, was wearing a Japanese flag headband and lime green sweatbands on his wrists. He almost scored on a breakaway, but Ian made a great save and threw the ball to Goran.

Riley raced to get back. It was going to be close. Goran arrived first, but Riley was right behind him. As Riley approached, Goran shielded him off the ball, frustrating Riley so much he pushed Goran in the back. Coach Anderson started to call a foul, but Goran barely moved. He kept shielding Riley, carried the ball forward, and blasted a shot past JoJo.

As Goran ran back, he passed right beside Riley and gave

him a shoulder bump. Riley turned and began shouting in Goran's face. Goran just laughed.

Riley raised a fist. The whistle blew as Kenji ran over and wrapped his arms around his teammate. Samantha had a long talk with Riley, while Coach Anderson took Goran aside.

The rest of the game, Goran and Riley fought like hungry badgers, tackling each other hard, tugging jerseys, and trying to level each other with shoulder charges. Goran couldn't beat him one v one because Riley was too fast and good, but Riley had trouble stealing the ball from Goran because he's so big and strong.

Riley finally got the ball on a breakaway. His rattail flying, he flew past Goran and then dashed by Otto. I thought Riley's next touch was a little out of control, but he managed to slide and toe the ball into the back of the net a nanosecond before Ian arrived.

Otto scored next on a smart chip from Goran that allowed Otto to head the ball over Kenji.

2–1.

After a long spell in which neither team had a good chance, Kenji intercepted a pass from Goran and made a quick pass to Riley, who gave it right back. Kenji fired a waist-high bullet past Ian to tie the game, then thrust a fist in the air, shouting a battle cry in Japanese.

Both teams fought hard for the final goal. I thought Riley had won the game, but he missed a hard left-footed shot by an inch. Otto's header hit the crossbar, and Kenji sent a flying scissor-kick all the way to Manchester.

In the end, Goran won the game by smacking a simple one-touch shot into the bottom left corner. Otto had set him up perfectly with a clever behind-the-leg pass. JoJo had no chance, but she hit the goalpost in disgust anyway. She didn't like to lose to Goran any more than the rest of us.

As Ajay and Emile walked out, ready for our semifinal game, Dmitri turned to me and smirked. "This should be easy."

"Don't be so sure," I replied. "They're both very good."

Dmitri sniffed. "You stay with Emile, I cover Ajay. He has no moves."

I shrugged. "We can try that."

Right from the start, I could tell Emile wanted to test me. When Ajay passed him the ball at kickoff, Emile drove right at me. He hesitated, trying to throw me off balance, then pushed the ball past me and tried to run on to it.

But I was ready. I shouldered him aside, recovered the ball, passed back to Ian, then turned and ran upfield. Ian kicked the ball long, laying it at my feet. I took one touch, then fired a shot through JoJo's legs at close range.

I patted her on the back. "Sorry. It was wide open."

"Get out of here, Leo."

As I jogged past Emile, he wouldn't look me in the eye.

They kicked off again. This time, Ajay tried to beat Dmitri down the sideline, and almost succeeded. But Dmitri poked the ball out of bounds.

Over the next few minutes, Dmitri tried again and again to beat Ajay, but my friend held his own. It was a good battle.

JoJo blocked a hard shot and threw the ball to Emile. This time, he tried a spin move I read from a mile away. *Does he think I'm a cupcake on defense? Or is he just that cocky?* Anyway, I stripped the ball and saw Dmitri taking off down the center. I sent a pass ahead of him, allowing the Russian striker to crush the ball into the side netting.

2–0.

On the next play, Emile and Ajay worked the ball downfield. Emile fed his partner a nice pass in front of the goal, just ahead of Dmitri. Ajay took a shot that Ian dove and saved.

Emile threw up his arms. "C'mon! That was an easy goal!"

"Hey!" Samantha snapped. "Stay positive or stay off the field."

I heard Emile mutter, "Whatever," too low for Samantha to hear.

Sure, Ajay should have made that shot. But Emile had made mistakes, too.

Ian threw the ball to Dmitri, but he lost it out of bounds. The next time I got the ball, Emile barked at Ajay to cover me. I wasn't sure why. Maybe Emile was tired of guarding me or thought he could dribble past Dmitri.

But they had to get the ball first, and I didn't think Emile could stick with Dmitri on a breakaway. I dribbled around the center of the field for a bit, evading Ajay and looking for an opening. Once I saw Dmitri cut towards the goal, I turned and whipped a pass downfield, letting him and Emile race for the ball.

Dmitri won by a full step and slipped a low shot past JoJo. The Russian striker held up three fingers as he ran back.

Emile turned on Ajay. "You're terrible. Why'd you let Leo make that pass?"

Instead of putting his head down, Ajay snapped back. "Me? Dmitri just smoked you. And Leo embarrassed you all game."

Samantha blew the whistle. "Both of you—three Carolinas, now. Coach Anderson, will you watch them? Then we'll have a little chat after the tournament."

Ajay threw up his hands as if to say, *Why me?* Then he saw the storm clouds gathering on Samantha's face and walked away, hanging his head.

Samantha grabbed the ball. "Alright, everyone. It's time for the final! Who's going to win the coveted Knights tracksuits?"

"Three to one Yank's team wins," Brock said.

Goran stared him down. "I will take that bet. How much money do you have?"

Brock laughed. "Yeah, good luck, bloke."

As I jogged out, wishing Brock wouldn't make such a big deal of it, I realized my legs were feeling much worse than before, like ice picks were stuck inside the backs of my heels, jabbing me with every step. I grimaced and forced the pain away. It wasn't like I was skipping the final. I would just have to deal with it.

Otto put a toe on the ball and wiped sweat off his large forehead. We fist bumped each other, and I could tell he was tired. So was our team. Unlike Goran, Dmitri and I had played two games in a row. That wasn't fair at all.

Stop making excuses. Get out there and play.

Samantha blew the whistle.

Otto kicked off to Goran.

The championship was on.

"You take Goran," Dmitri said, knowing I was the better defender.

"Okay."

The Serbian midfielder came straight at me. I was surprised, knowing one v one isn't his game. I leaned down, put one foot forward, and shifted my weight to the balls of my toes.

Just before I dove in, Goran passed the ball, then ran straight into me, throwing me hard to the ground.

Samantha called the foul. "Goran, what was that?"

"Sorry. I lost my balance."

"That isn't what it looked like."

He reached down, offering me a hand. As I accepted the gesture, I saw a cruel gleam in his eye and knew he had done that on purpose.

I limped forward to take the kick. When I tried to hit Dmitri on the run, Otto made a nice stop, then shielded Dmitri and turned upfield. This happened a lot over the next portion of the game. Goran and Otto knew how to use their size to their advantage. If the field was longer, Dmitri and I could have used our speed, but we had to deal with what we had.

After dancing with the ball, Dmitri tried to beat Otto down the wing. Otto stuck out a foot and stripped him. Then he carried it downfield, forcing me to swing over, and passed to Goran right in front of the goal. Goran took a shot. JoJo got a hand on the ball, but it was too hard and went through her fingers.

Goran turned towards Brock on the sideline and made the score with his fingers. 1–0.

Brock snarled and crossed his arms.

I toed the ball at the center circle, ready to fight back. When Samantha blew the whistle, I gave the ball to Dmitri, who returned it and took off. I feigned a long pass then cut hard to my left. Goran stumbled, unable to hang with the speed of my move. He regained his footing, but not before I had pushed past him, driving forward with Dmitri on my right.

Otto did his best to stay between us. As he edged towards me, trying to cut off my shooting angle, I faked another pass to Dmitri, then swung to my left again. Otto bit hard on the fake, leaving me racing towards the goal. Still annoyed by Goran's foul, I slammed the ball in the top left corner, giving Ian no chance to save it.

This time, Brock held up a finger on each hand.

Goran stomped to the center line and waited on Ian to fish the ball out of the net. As Goran breathed, the muscles in his chest rose and fell, pushing against his practice jersey. His thick arms were tanned from the sun and sweat dripped down his heavy dark brow. I think the guy's neck was as big as my whole torso.

Normally guys that size tire easily. But not Goran. As the game went on, his pace never slowed. Every time I got the ball, he was right in my face, daring me to go by him, trying to prove a point to the coaches.

JoJo made a save and tossed the ball to Dmitri. He started towards Otto then passed to me in the middle. The pass was a little short. When I ran to get it, I saw Goran coming on hard. There was no time to turn. All I could do was reach the ball and toe it forward. As I made the quick pass to Dmitri, Goran rammed me with his shoulder, again sending me to the turf. I sprawled face-first in the grass. Everyone booed on the sideline, but Samantha opened her palms, signaling a fair charge.

I pulled myself to my feet as Goran and Otto played a nice combo that turned Dmitri around and made him look silly.

Goran took a hard shot that JoJo barely saved, soaring to her left and landing with a thump on the ground.

"C'mon," she said. "My gran kicks harder than that."

As she threw me the ball, Goran snarled and chased me downfield. I spied Dmitri curling around Otto and sent a long pass that skipped once and landed at his feet. All Dmitri had to do was make the trap, but the ball bounced off his foot, allowing Otto to retrieve it.

Now they had a breakaway. I veered towards Otto, forcing him to pass. When he did, I slid and intercepted the ball. I jumped to my feet as Goran ran in. We both tried to kick the ball at the same time. I was angry and put all my strength into my kick, trying to push through his foot, win the ball, and knock him off balance.

Instead, Goran's leg swept through mine like a lawnmower through a patch of grass. The ball went flying, and so did I, landing on my back as a shockwave of pain went through my leg. I stumbled to my feet and tried to chase the ball down, but it was too late. Otto and Goran had another breakaway. This time they made it count.

2–1.

I walked back to the center of the field, gritted my teeth, and kicked off to Dmitri. Then I curled around him, calling for the ball. He led me down the sideline. Otto gave chase, but I took one touch and blew by him. As I cut inside, trying to get a good angle, Goran thundered over. I tried a hard shot, but it was too far out, and Ian saved it. I chastised myself for not trying to get closer, and knew I was worried about getting flattened again.

Playing scared.

"Go!" Goran roared, hitting a long ball to Otto.

Dmitri raced back in time to block the shot. He passed to me, and I received the ball with Goran on my back.

"Come on, Leo," he taunted. "Take me on."

Okay, then. I will. As his back pressed against me, trying to bully me off the ball, I spun left and flicked the ball between his tree trunk legs, nutmegging him. I curled around him and was about to explode forward when he threw his hip into mine, knocking me to the ground.

Samantha blew the whistle. "Take it down a notch, Goran. He's your teammate."

Goran raised his hands. "What? I thought it was a fair challenge."

"It was a hip check, and this isn't hockey."

Samantha set the ball down. I was breathing hard and hurting all over. My left hip felt like someone had smashed it with a hammer.

"Leo!" Dmitri cried and took off running.

I slipped the free kick between Goran and Otto, but Ian came out to run it down. Dmitri, knowing he didn't have time to shoot, one-touched the ball back to me, right in front of Goran. Was Dmitri trying to kill me? I tried to turn, but Goran threw his body to the ground and slide-tackled me, the ball, and a giant clod of grass.

As I lay on my back, chest heaving, Samantha walked over to me. "Leo," she said quietly. "Are you okay?"

I nodded, gritted my teeth, and pushed to my feet.

On the next play, when Dmitri passed me the ball, I turned and burst towards the goal, eager to tie the score. Goran and Otto both stepped up. I started to pass to Dmitri, who was streaking upfield, then pushed the ball forward, fooling everyone. Goran grunted and made a grab at my jersey. I shook him off and rocketed a shot on goal.

Smack!

Ian's large hands blocked it. If that had been a regulation-size goal, I would have scored.

The next ball went to Goran. I met him at midfield and pressed into his back, determined to fight. But he kept moving me towards my own goal, pushing hard with his back and rolling the ball forward with the bottom of his foot. I tried to get around him, but he used his arms and big body to keep me away. It was so frustrating. Finally, he passed to Otto and curled around me. He gave me a little shove as well, just enough to knock me back a step. Then he burst into open space, calling for the ball in his deep voice. "Here!"

Otto held off Dmitri and swung his foot back for a cross. I scrambled to get back. As the ball dropped from the sky, Goran backed into me again, using his body to keep me away.

The ball had almost landed. I nudged and bumped and even pushed him in the small of his back, using all my strength to try and move him. If he got the ball first, he would have an easy shot.

But nothing worked. Goran kept me safely behind him as he trapped the ball on his chest and let it hit the ground. Then he shrugged me off with ease, took one dribble, and slammed the ball into the bottom right corner.

As I sank to the ground, aching and exhausted, Goran patted me on the shoulder like I was a little kid who needed comforting. Then he turned towards Brock, thrust a hand in the air, and held up three fingers.

ENTRY #16

Answers

After the game, I limped off the field, hurting all over. It wasn't just my body. My pride was wounded, too.

I knew it shouldn't mean that much. It was only a friendly two v two tourney with my teammates.

Except it wasn't that friendly, and the final game *had* meant something.

Goran had taken the challenge personally and decided to prove a point to the coaches. Sure, he had fouled me a few times, but overall, he had gotten the better of me, and his team had won the game.

Maybe he was the better player.

Even worse, deep down, I knew I was a little bit afraid of him.

As Samantha handed out the tracksuits to the winners, Brock clapped me on the shoulder. "You were robbed, Yank. That cheating bloke fouled you all over the field."

Dmitri approached me next. "It's okay, yes? We did good. Goran is very strong player."

I didn't respond to either of them.

⚽ ⚽ ⚽

Later that night, I woke to a severe leg cramp. Has that ever happened to you? It's awful. I shouted in pain, rolled off the bed onto the floor, and tried desperately to straighten my leg. It took a long time, but finally the cramp calmed down. But I had trouble sleeping through the night and was tired when I woke.

Before practice, Samantha gathered us around and showed us the table. So far, everyone had played ten games. The Dragons were 8–1–1 and had 25 points. They were in first place but not by much.

Liverpool and the Oxford Royals were tied for second with 23 points.

Our record was 7–1–2. Seven wins, one loss to the Dragons, and two ties. We had 22 points and were in fourth place, only three points below the top.

"You're doing great," Samantha said. "Keep it up. We still have to play two of the top three teams before the break, but so do the Dragons. We could even take the lead by the halfway point of the season."

A cheer broke out among the players.

"We've got a lot of work to do," she continued. "Let's have a strong week of practice and beat Brighton this weekend. One game at a time, Knights. One game at a time."

⚽   ⚽   ⚽

My legs hurt at the start of practice and got worse the longer we played. That night, I had more leg cramps, and they returned the next night as well.

By the end of practice on Friday, I could barely walk off the field. The pain was awful, much sharper than before. Every time I tried to kick or run it felt like someone was twisting a knife into my Achilles tendons.

My friends had all noticed and asked me what was wrong. I shrugged them off, telling them I'd be fine, but I wasn't sure how I would manage to play in the game tomorrow.

On the walk back to my room, Samantha came up beside me and touched my elbow. "Come on, Leo. You're coming with me."

I swallowed from the pain and looked up. "I am? Where?"

"To see the team physio."

⚽ ⚽ ⚽

Andrew Nunn, the trainer and physical therapist who looked after the Knights Academy players, was tending to an injury on a practice field when we entered the waiting room of his office next to the school.

A physical therapist isn't quite the same as a medical doctor. They specialize in sports injuries and help people heal with exercises and stretching and strength training.

Mr. Nunn returned in fifteen minutes, sat down with me and Samantha, and asked what the trouble was. He was about forty years old and wearing black Knights sweatpants, a green polo shirt, and a visor.

"My legs," I mumbled. "They hurt."

"A little or a lot?"

I glanced at Samantha. "A lot."

"Which parts of your legs?"

"Pretty much all the parts. But mostly the lower."

"I see. When do they hurt?"

"Pretty much all the time."

"Hmm. Is it worse when you play?"

I nodded. "Especially when I run. And kick."

"Those two bits are rather important to a footballer, aren't they?"

I hung my head, afraid of what he might tell me. Did I have some terrible disease? Were my pro dreams about to be flushed down the toilet?

Mr. Nunn was standing next to a long, padded table, similar to the ones in doctors' offices. He patted the table and asked me to hop onto it. After I did, he probed my leg muscles for a bit, then asked me to flex them in different positions as his fingers continued digging.

"Ow," I said, gripping the table when he touched the back of my right Achilles tendon. He moved to the left one, and I winced again. Same with both my heels.

Beside me, I saw Samantha's hands clench, and I knew she was worried. I was glad she was here.

Mr. Nunn asked me to walk around the room. He watched me, then stepped back and crossed his arms. "How long has this been going on?"

"Most of the season," I said. "It wasn't that bad in the beginning."

"It's getting worse?"

I nodded again.

He asked me to take a seat beside Samantha. Then he stroked his chin and sat in a chair beside me. "I'm going to send you to the orthopedist for a second opinion. But I'm almost certain I know what's going on. Leo, I believe you have Sever's disease."

I knew it. I just knew it. I have a terrible disease that will probably cause my legs to rot away and fall off within months.

Not only will my future soccer career be ruined, but I might never walk again.

"What," I croaked, barely able to get the words out, "is Sever's disease?"

I couldn't even look at Samantha, afraid of the pity I would see.

"Sever's disease," Mr. Nunn said, "is a condition when the growth plates in the back of the heels are active and become inflamed due to overuse. In layman's terms, Sever's disease is a fancy diagnosis for acute growing pains."

I reeled, feeling as if my chair had been yanked out from under me, unprepared for the terrible shock of the—

Wait, what?

Growing pains?

"Growing pains?" I repeated out loud.

"It's rather common at your age," he said. "Well, not the severity of yours, but millions of young people suffer aches and pains when their bodies change and develop. The natural growing process is more painful for some than others, and it can be aggravated by strain or heavy exercise. This is especially true among elite athletes, as you can imagine. It's one of the more common complaints I see at the Academy."

"Oh," I said, embarrassed that nothing was truly wrong with me.

"I can see what you're thinking, and don't be ashamed. Sever's disease can be *very* painful. In fact, since yours is so acute—those Achilles are quite sensitive—I'm surprised you're still on the pitch. Have you been practicing and playing every day?"

"Oh yes," Samantha said in a tight voice. "Leo hasn't

missed a beat. I've seen him wincing for some time, and I'm kicking myself for not coming in earlier." She turned to me. "Why didn't you say anything?"

"Because I didn't want to sit," I said weakly.

Mr. Nunn chuckled. "I get that a lot. Unfortunately, you're gonna have to give those legs a break."

I swallowed. "For how long?"

"Now that I can't tell you. We can try orthopedic inserts for your shoes, and some pain medicine, but the only true cure for Sever's disease is rest. With most people, the pain goes away in a few weeks or months, and they're never bothered again."

"Months?" I echoed in a small voice. "Could it . . . could it take even longer?"

"In severe cases, the pain can last two years or more."

Two years? I felt dizzy all of a sudden. If I had to sit out that long, it could ruin my entire future. "So which one . . . which one do I have? A severe one or a not severe one?"

"That's impossible to say. Everyone's growth trajectory varies. It could be that you're going through a quick growth spurt, and this will pass soon enough. In fact, that's the more likely scenario. But I'll be honest and tell you we can't be sure until you give it some time. It all depends on what your body decides to do."

I hung my head again. "How long do I have to sit?"

"Here's the thing. You don't *have* to sit out. Sever's disease isn't an injury in that sense. But it will *hurt*. And until it calms down, the more you push yourself, the worse it will get. You don't want to get to the point where you can't walk, which I've seen in extreme cases."

"But there's a game tomorrow," I said. "My team needs me."

"I strongly advise you to skip that game."

Samantha leaned forward. "What's your advice moving forward?"

Mr. Nunn looked me in the eye. "Rest for a week and see how you feel. If the pain goes away, try to play and see what happens. If it starts hurting again, stop for another week. You'll know when you can train fully again. Your body will tell you."

I slumped in my chair, terrified I would have Sever's disease for two years and miss a super important period in my development and never make another Prem youth team.

Someone knocked on the door. Dr. Nunn checked his watch and said, "I'll prescribe some medicine for the pain and refer you to our ortho. I'm really sorry about this, but you know, there is a silver lining."

My eyes slowly lifted. "There is? What?"

"The presence of growing pains indicates, well, that you're growing."

ENTRY #17

Ups and Downs

After leaving Mr. Nunn's office, Samantha patted my shoulder and told me everything would be fine. That I just needed to rest a bit, heal up, and I'd be back on the field in no time.

I wasn't so sure.

When I returned to my room, the first thing I did was look in the mirror. Had I really grown? I couldn't tell. My puny muscles looked the same as always. My shoes felt tight, but I guessed that was because my feet were inflamed from the pain.

Huh. Maybe I had moved up a size.

Next I marked the top of my head on the wall with a pencil. I didn't have a tape measure, but I had a ruler in my desk. I took it out and carefully measured my height.

I'd grown an inch and a half since summer.

Wow. Okay. Didn't expect that.

I let out a deep breath, full of conflicted emotions. Though worried about my future, I *was* glad I was growing. For a while I thought I'd be the same height the rest of my life.

Now I just needed to gain some muscle—and not grow too fast, so I could get back on the field.

⚽ ⚽ ⚽

The next morning, I watched from the sideline as my teammates ran out against the Brighton Barkers. My friends knew about my growing pains and told me how much the team needed me. But it was still really hard. I wanted to be on that field so much.

Watching Goran start at center mid was even harder.

Along with that change, Samantha put Ian in the goal instead of JoJo.

"We'll see how that overgrown frog does," JoJo said. She was sitting next to me on the bench. "Who wears a bright green jersey, anyway? And so what if he's better with his feet? I block shots. That's what keepers do, innit?"

"Yeah," I said. "I'd take you back there any day."

Ajay was sitting on my other side. "One hundred percent," he said. "Coach Anderson loves Ian. I know that's why he's out there."

JoJo snorted. "He loves Goran and Dmitri, too. Isn't there some kinda law against that? Giving everything to your family and friends?"

I didn't respond because I didn't think they were right. Coach Anderson might have some influence with Samantha, but she made her own decisions.

Brighton was a mid-table team, tenth in the league. They had a good midfield with twin brothers who Otto said were from Istanbul, Turkey. They worked really well together, but Otto and Goran held them in check in the first half. By halftime, neither team had scored, and both our coaches said we needed more possession.

"We have to play out of the back," Coach Anderson insisted. "We're giving away the ball too cheaply. We've practiced these situations all week. Riley and Brock, you've got Ian back there now. He's good with his feet. Use him."

Beside me, JoJo muttered something too low for anyone to hear.

"One change," Samantha said. "Kenji, you're in for Duncan. All right, Knights. We're knocking on the door. Push hard this half and I know good things will happen."

Not long into the second period, Marco made a driving run down the wing. He earned a corner kick and whipped a ball into the penalty box. There was a battle for the header, which Goran won by storming inside and bullying his way to the ball. His shot slipped through the goalie's hands and into the back of the net.

After that, the game went back and forth for a while without any shots on goal. But as time ran out, the Barkers goalie blocked Patrick's attempt and started a counterattack.

The ball sailed down the sideline. When their left winger tried to beat Kenji one v one, Kenji knocked the ball loose with a slide tackle. The winger recovered and kept dribbling. Riley swung over. He drove his foot hard into the tackle, popping the ball loose. The striker raced over to recover it. Riley stole it back, but the striker pressured him hard.

Normally Riley would boot the ball upfield. But now, knowing he was supposed to keep possession, he turned this way and that, trying to find someone to pass to. No one was open except Ian, so Riley sent the ball back to our keeper. All game long, Ian had done a good job getting the ball upfield.

But this time, the right winger guessed what Riley would do, and was racing inside. Before the pass reached Ian, the winger dove in and kicked the ball straight into the goal.

On the sideline, Coach Anderson threw down his clipboard. Riley, furious with himself, grabbed the ball out of the net and kicked it into the stands. This earned him a yellow card and a scolding from Samantha.

We pressed hard for the last few minutes, but we couldn't get another goal. The game ended in a 1–1 tie.

Riley left the field with his head hanging low, and Samantha made him run Carolinas for losing his temper.

⚽ ⚽ ⚽

I rested the whole week. My legs felt much better when I woke up on Saturday morning. I told Samantha I wanted to play, and she agreed to let me.

I'd missed practice all week and didn't expect to start the game against the Devonshire Demons. So I was surprised when Samantha called my name—and put me at center mid.

I was also stunned when Kenji's name was called instead of Riley's.

Kenji had been playing really well, and he deserved a chance, but Riley was an amazing defender.

Was this really the right decision?

I ran out to my position, though without Riley and Ajay and JoJo, it almost felt like I was playing on a different team.

The day was cool and windy and clear. It was four p.m. in late November, so the sun was already sinking, and the second half would be played under the lights. Everyone except Duncan wore long sleeves under their jerseys. Some people even wore gloves and leggings. But Duncan ran out in shorts and a T-shirt, pumping his thick legs and blowing into his hands. I guess he was from some snowy place in Scotland and didn't mind the cold.

Though we all were disappointed by the tie game against the Barkers, the Dragons and Liverpool had also tied, and so had the Royals and the Marauders. None of the top teams had gained any points on us.

The whistle blew. As the game started, I ran around with lots of energy, cutting and weaving and feinting, feeling better than I had in weeks. I had three shots on goal and made a sweet pass to Patrick, which led to a goal by Dmitri. I didn't get credit for the assist, but it was a good pass that led to the only goal of the first forty-five minutes.

Everything was going great until the ref blew the whistle to end the half. As I walked off the field, my adrenaline drained away and my growing pains returned. I gritted my teeth and tried not to let it show, determined to finish the game.

But the pain continued into the second half. I began to tire, too. I hadn't practiced all week, and, in top level soccer, you lose game endurance pretty quickly if you don't stay in shape.

Samantha noticed and took me out. I didn't blame her.

On my way to the bench, she kept her eyes on the game but said, "How are you feeling, Leo?"

"Okay."

"Just okay? Tell me the truth."

I took a deep breath. "Great for the first half. In the second, my legs hurt."

"Thought so. Get some rest, okay? You played really well."

Five minutes later, Goran scored off a free kick, his second goal in two games.

With twenty minutes to go, Samantha subbed Riley for Duncan, and when the score was 3–0, with only five minutes left, she put Ajay in for Marco.

We had won the game, but I didn't think we looked our best. There were too many changes in the squad.

When Samantha took over from Coach Purcell, we had transitioned from an old school kick-and-run style to Samantha's more modern strategy. I knew she was doing the same thing this season. Trying to adapt her style and improve the team. But right now, everything felt jumbled.

And, even if we did get better, where did my friends and I fit in?

⚽   ⚽   ⚽

Later that night, I noticed Riley wasn't in the cafeteria for dinner. He had seemed down all week. When Samantha had chosen Kenji to start over him, I could tell Riley was crushed. Soccer was everything to him. I mean, we all lived and breathed the game, but I had the feeling, since Riley didn't seem to have any friends or family that cared about him, it meant even more to him.

After dinner, I went to his room to check on him. He didn't answer the door and he didn't have a phone.

Still, I wasn't too worried. I figured he didn't want to talk or was out walking around. In fact, a few of us—me, Brock, Patrick, and Otto—decided to go for a walk around Lewisham. It was Saturday night, and we had a sudden craving for gelato. After signing out, we walked three blocks to our favorite gelateria, chatted for a while, and took our time coming back. As we approached the entrance to the Caravan, we were surprised to see a police car pulling up to the curb right in front of the tall iron gates. We stopped walking, unsure what was happening.

The doors to the police car opened. Two officers wearing bright green vests beneath their wool coats stepped out. One of the officers, a heavyset man with a beard, opened a rear door to let out a passenger. At first I couldn't see who it was because the officer leaned down and took the passenger by the arm, as if to make sure they didn't run away. No doubt someone was in trouble.

As the passenger stepped out, guided by the officer towards the entrance to the Academy, I finally caught a glimpse of his face.

It was Riley.

ENTRY #18

Brock Party

"Hey!" Brock said. "Where are you taking our friend?"

The police officers ignored him, but Riley turned towards us with a defiant sneer. He stepped away from the officer but didn't try to run.

At that moment, Samantha came hurrying out of the administrative building. She must have been working late. "What's going on?" she said, meeting Riley and the officers at the front gate.

The officer with Riley stepped forward. "This lad vandalized a wall in Crystal Palace Park. Sprayed graffiti all over it. He gave us this address. Is he one of your players?"

"Yes," Samantha said, then turned towards Riley with a furious expression. "What were you thinking?"

"It was just the Moonies," he mumbled.

"What?"

"Moonchester and Moonbeam. Man City's mascots."

Brock barked a laugh, causing Samantha to glare at us. "You think this is a joke? Were any of you involved in this?"

As we quickly shook our heads, Riley said, "They had nuttin' to do with it."

"It was just the one," the bearded police officer confirmed.

Samantha pointed at the gated entrance. "You four—inside."

Brock, Patrick, Otto, and I hurried forward. As we passed Riley, he hung his head and stared at the pavement. Just before we entered the building, I heard Samantha and the two officers talking to Riley in angry tones, but I couldn't hear what they were saying.

⚽ ⚽ ⚽

The next day, at morning conditioning, Samantha announced that Riley was suspended from the team for damaging public property. "I don't know when he'll be back," she said. "Or *if* he'll be back. That will be up to the youth court and Riley himself."

"Is he going to jail?" I asked quietly.

"I don't think his crime was that serious, but it's possible he could go to a juvenile detention center. For now, he's staying here. He'll be in class with you today. Let's not make him feel bad, okay? Everyone makes mistakes, and it's our job to support him and get him through it."

⚽ ⚽ ⚽

At practice, Samantha asked me to sit out if my legs were hurting. They did hurt, so I barely played all week, and my conditioning got worse and worse.

Our next game was in Oxford against the Royals. After Friday's practice, Samantha took me aside. "Leo, I want to tell you something."

I knew, by the look in her eye, what she was about to say. "I'm not starting tomorrow, am I?"

"You're starting, just not in the middle."

"Oh."

"I'm playing you on the right and Goran in the middle. If you want to play, that is. If you don't, I understand."

"No, I . . . I want to play."

"Okay. But have you thought about resting until you heal completely? Even if it takes the rest of the season?"

Of course I'd thought about it, but I was terrified I'd fall behind. "I'll be fine."

She gave me a long look. "We'll see how it goes and evaluate day by day. If I don't think you should continue, I'm pulling you out."

"I understand." There was a question I had to ask. "If you think I'm okay to start . . . why aren't I in the middle?"

She got a pained look in her eye. "Leo, you're playing really well. Even with your injury. And I know it's affecting your fitness. We can't play our best if we're not in shape, right? But since you asked, I want to be honest, because you know I tell it like it is. At this point in time, Coach Anderson and I feel that Goran is just a little bit ahead of you. Not in talent but in physical development."

"You mean he's bigger and stronger."

"He holds the ball really well, and he's been scoring. Even in the Premier League, stars hit a wall sometimes, and another player might take their place for a while. *Everyone* comes off the bench at some point in their career. Hang in there, okay? I know you're going through a tough time right now."

I looked off to the side. "Okay."

⚽ ⚽ ⚽

The Oxford Royals were tied for second in the table. The game started at one p.m., and Oxford is about two hours from London, so we headed out right after breakfast on Saturday morning.

There was another change to the lineup: Kenji started in place of Riley and played amazing in the first half. He shut down every attack on his side and carried the ball forward really well.

I played fine but didn't stand out. It was strange being on the right. I wasn't used to the position. It hurt my confidence a little, as did my lack of conditioning and the fear that my growing pains would erupt at any moment. In my heart, I knew I wasn't taking risks on the field or playing anywhere near my potential.

At halftime, the score was 0–0. Not long into the second half, Goran scored off a pass from Marco. Otto had done most of the work, setting up Marco with a great chip over the defense. Then Marco raced around a defender and passed the ball to Goran right in front of the goal.

Almost anyone could have tapped it in—but I had to give Goran credit for making the run and putting himself in a good position.

Not long after, my Achilles started throbbing, and I was forced to ask for a sub.

When the final whistle blew, the score was still 1–0. We had been lucky to escape with a win. It was a hard-fought battle, and the Royals missed a couple of easy chances, but Goran's goal made the difference.

A great victory against the second-place team.

⚽ ⚽ ⚽

Later in the day, my friends and I took the London Overground to Brock's house for his fourteenth birthday party. He had invited the entire team. Even Goran and Dmitri came. Only Riley stayed behind, though we all knocked on his door and shouted at him to join us. He had barely spoken to anyone since the night the police brought him home. Every day after class, when the rest of us headed to practice, Riley shuffled alone to his building with his head down. I felt so bad for him. I knew he had vandalized that wall because he lost his starting position.

After a long journey, we all exited at the Dalston-Kingsland stop. That's a neighborhood in northeast London, in the London borough of Hackney. In case you're wondering, the closest Premier League teams are West Ham, Arsenal, and Tottenham. But Brock's parents are from Liverpool and that's who his family supports.

I'd always been curious to see where Brock lives. His townhome was on a street lined with similar homes that sat side-by-side, all the way up and down the street, with no space in between. That's normal in London.

The homes were all two- or three-stories high, built from beige or brown bricks, and had tiny front yards with large windows facing the street. On the inside, Brock's house was a little chilly but full of people and laughter. Family photos and knickknacks covered the walls and shelves. The maroon carpet looked about a hundred years old, and I could tell they had cats by the smell.

Brock had a large family, and they were all built sturdy like him. Even his mom and sisters. Brock was the oldest and largest sibling, but he was only half the size of his dad, who resembled a refrigerator with legs.

"Come in," his father roared, pumping our hands one by one as we entered the long hallway just inside the house. He had a red face with a bristly moustache, a fat square head like Brock's, and a belly even rounder than Coach Beppe's.

The kitchen was the last room on the floor. Brock's mother was drinking tea at a table with snacks set out, along with a giant red cake with Liverpool written in white icing. A Liverpool banner hung from the wall, and even the presents had Liverpool wrapping.

After greeting us, Brock's mother opened a glass door that led to a little garden with a bed of flowers and a pair of soccer goals set up. Two of Brock's sisters were kicking a ball around.

We all took a paper plate, filled up on snacks, and gathered around a pair of picnic tables in the garden. Soon after we arrived, Brock's father left to pick up fish and chips for everyone.

No one was surprised that Brock had chosen fish and chips for his birthday dinner.

For the first few hours, we had a great time. We juggled in the garden, then listened to some of Brock's terrible music in his bedroom (which was covered with Liverpool swag and posters). When his dad returned, we devoured the fish and chips—the best I've ever had—then tore through the cake like a pack of starving coyotes.

"Blimey!" his mother said. "I should've gotten two."

Brock burped and patted his belly. "Delicious cake, Mummy."

After the party ended, Brock walked everyone back to the

Overground stop. So far, everyone had gotten along, though Goran and his friends had kept to themselves. Eventually we started talking about the team and our chances of winning the title.

"We're only three points behind the Dragons," Duncan said.

"True," Otto replied, "but we'll have to *beat* the Dragons to win the league."

Emile threw up a hand. "Is this guy always so negative?"

"The stats aren't in our favor," Otto declared. "And we still have to play Liverpool twice."

"We'll be fine," Goran said in his thick Serbian accent. He talked slowly and his voice was always full of confidence. "Now that I'm the center mid."

All of a sudden, everyone grew quiet. I felt very small and wanted to disappear.

Brock snorted. "Whatever, bloke. The only reason you're starting at the ten is because Leo has growing pains."

A few people snickered. Goran stopped walking and turned to face Brock.

"I don't think so," Goran said in that same cocky tone. "We all know who the better player is. Don't we, Leo?" He turned towards me. "Remember the two v two? But you're a very good player. I'm glad you're on my right."

My face felt as red and hot as a furnace. I didn't even know what to say. He was being a jerk, but I couldn't deny the truth of it. I wanted to lash out at him and took a step forward with my fists balled at my sides. I wasn't going to hit him or anything, but I was just so mad.

Goran walked right up to me, chest to chest, daring me to try something.

Brock pushed us apart. "Why'd I invite you, anyway?" he said to Goran.

He slapped Brock's hand away. "I don't know. It was a bad idea."

After staring Brock down, Goran backed away and started walking towards the Overground station. His best friends—Dmitri and Ian and Emile—hurried to catch up with him. With a shrug, Marco left, too, though he walked slowly by himself with his hands in his pockets.

I stood in the middle of the sidewalk, embarrassed and furious. As we started towards the station again, Brock fell into step beside me. "Hey, Yank, remember how you shut me up once? At the Dragons camp?"

I gritted my teeth, so upset I felt jittery all over. "Yeah," I mumbled. "On the field."

"That's right. On the field. You're a better player than Goran. He needs a lesson, too."

My friends all echoed his opinion, which made me feel warm inside.

But I wasn't convinced they were right.

ENTRY #19

Tig the Superstar

In December, we played two more games before Christmas break. We won the first but lost to Liverpool 2–1.

Despite the tough loss, most of our team played well. Goran had another strong game, and Patrick scored off an assist from Dmitri. Although Kenji did great at center back, I missed having Riley back there.

In the goal, Ian made some great passes, but I thought he should have saved one of Liverpool's shots. But he was half a step too slow, and the ball bounced off his glove and into the net.

When Christmas break started, we were in fourth place, now six points behind the Dragons. Diego and Aron led the league in goals, and José had the most assists.

On the bright side, we were doing much better than at this time last year.

On the not-so-bright side, in the last two games, I had only played one half. I didn't have a single goal or assist or even a great play. I was getting more and more out of shape, and my growing pains were messing with my head.

Would I ever be the same player?

⚽ ⚽ ⚽

The day after Christmas break started, I was the last person left in our building. Well, maybe Riley was still there, but I hadn't heard from him, and he still wasn't answering his door or showing up in the cafeteria. I think he was surviving on granola bars.

My flight home left early the next morning. After lunch—it was strange eating by myself in the cafeteria—Samantha saw me juggling alone on the field.

She wandered over. "How are the legs?"

I put a foot on the ball. "Not bad today."

"Glad to hear it. Say, Leo, I know your flight's in the morning, but do you have any plans tonight?"

"Nope."

"Want to come see Tig's game with me?"

My eyes bugged. "Uh, yeah!"

"Thought you might. They're playing Crystal Palace, so it's close. Meet me in the front office at five?"

"You got it."

⚽ ⚽ ⚽

Later that evening, Samantha and I were sitting in the first row behind the Dragons U21 bench as Tig's game was about to start. He waved to us as he ran onto the field. I supposed I would have to root for the Dragons for one game.

Well, maybe I'd just root for Tig.

"I'm glad you came," Samantha said. "I'm sure Tig is, too."

"I've never seen him play. At least not in a game."

"Really?" She laughed. "I guess we keep you busy. And I know you've got a lot on your mind. I find the best way to take the pressure off myself is to focus on other people. Help them, support them, root for them."

I cheered wildly as Tig took off down the right wing, blowing by a defender. He was so *good*, as fast as the wind and smooth as butter with the ball. When the center back swung over, Tig teased him with a few body feints, took off down the line, and whipped a powerful cross into the middle. The Dragons striker rose to head the ball and just missed the goal.

"Ah!" I said, putting my hands against my head.

Samantha stood and clapped. "Way to work, Tig! Great cross!"

At halftime, the score was 0–0. I was very impressed by both teams. They looked like pros to my eyes. How much better did you have to be to get called up to the Prem?

Samantha left to buy popcorn and drinks. When she returned, the players were taking the field again. We snacked and chatted as the half started, and I asked if she thought Riley would rejoin the team.

"Funny you should ask," she replied, "because I just heard something today. The youth court has agreed to let him perform community service over the break instead of going to juvenile detention."

"That's great. Will he do that here or with his family?"

She pressed her lips together. "He's in Manchester."

I could tell she didn't think this was a positive development.

"If he performs his community service," she continued, "and stays out of trouble, he should be back in London in January."

"To rejoin the team?"

"Maybe. If I think he's ready." She looked off to the side. "He made a mistake, Leo. A pretty big one. But we all do, and everyone deserves a second chance. I've made plenty of mistakes this year."

"You have?"

"I know our team chemistry isn't the best. I blame myself for that."

"That isn't your fault. Some of us just don't get along."

"I'm not blind. I can see where the problems are. I'm just not sure what the answer is. I do know that to be at our best we have to work through it."

I asked a question that had been on my mind for a while. "Do you think I should quit? And come back next year?"

The Dragons surged downfield, and we stopped talking to watch. Tig put an amazing move on a defender—an inside scissor with his right foot, then a burst of speed to his left— and curved a pass into the box. The Dragons striker took a shot that just missed.

"Drat," Samantha said, then fell silent for a moment. "I don't know, Leo. I suppose it depends on how much pain you're in."

"I just don't want to fall behind."

"I understand," she said gently. "But maybe it's better to let yourself heal. Sometimes we have to take a step back so we can move forward."

I thought about that.

"Here's another piece of advice," she continued, "that helped me when I was injured. I was depressed because I couldn't play. My mom told me I should focus on what I *can* do, and not what I can't."

She jumped up and began yelling. "Go! Go!"

I whirled and saw Tig sprinting forward on a breakaway, just past the half line. Two Crystal Palace players were chasing him. Tig kicked the ball ahead, a perfect touch that allowed him to cut inside. The away crowd, Samantha and me included, were on our feet, cheering him on.

As fast as Tig was—and he was blindingly fast—I thought one of the defenders would catch him. It's hard to dribble half the length of the field by yourself, and defenders have an advantage because they're running without the ball. But Tig took another long touch and kept going, staying a step ahead.

I held my breath. It was obvious he wasn't going to pass. He wanted to finish the breakaway and score.

Twenty yards to go. The closest defender tried to grab Tig's shirt, but Tig shrugged him off. The defender stumbled and fell behind. Now it was Tig and the goalie, one v one.

The goalie raced out. Tig feinted left, then pushed the ball to the right with the outside of his foot. It was a simple but perfect move that gained him a step on the keeper. As the goalie scrambled to recover, Tig hit an easy shot into the center of the goal, giving the Dragons a 1–0 lead.

After the goal, Tig ran across the field and slid on his knees right in front of us. He looked straight at Samantha, blew her a kiss, then held his fist out to me in front of the whole crowd.

That proved to be the winning goal.

Tig was a superstar, and I just knew I'd see him in the Prem one day.

ENTRY #20

Home Sweet Home

I slept for most of the flight home. When I saw my dad in the airport, waiting for me at the departure gate, he eyed me up and down. "You've grown, kiddo."

"I have?"

"Two inches at least. You're filling out some, too. Are your shoes getting tight?"

"Yeah."

"We'll sort that out." He gave me a hug. "I'm glad you're home."

On the long ride to Ohio, I caught him up on our last few games but didn't tell him about Goran or that I'd been moved to right midfield. He didn't ask, and I was too embarrassed.

When we arrived at our house, Aunt Janice had a spaghetti dinner waiting. I'd never been so relieved to be home. After dinner, I collapsed on my bed, glad I didn't have to worry, at least for a few weeks, about growing pains or giant Serbian midfielders or losing my starting position.

I just needed a steady supply of home cooking, video games, and friend time.

"And Messi time," I said, walking over to my bearded dragon's cage.

The little guy was staring at me with his beady yellow eyes.

I could have sworn he had one eye cocked, as if to say, *Don't you have something to tell me?*

"Not you, too," I muttered. "I just want to chill."

Messi's beard flared, and he climbed to the top of his tree. Whatever.

Before I got ready for bed, I stood against the wall and measured myself. Dad was right—I'd grown another inch since last month!

No wonder I had growing pains.

I tried on some of my shirts from last year, and they didn't fit at all. My pants were short too. I took off my shirt and flexed in the mirror. Had I gained any muscle since the summer?

I couldn't tell a difference. If anything, I was stretched out and skinnier.

With a sigh, I hopped into bed and turned out the lights.

⚽ ⚽ ⚽

In the morning, I called up Carlos and Dennis and asked them to come over. It was great to see my old friends. The weather was awful—sleet pouring down—so we stayed inside and gamed all day. It was the weekend, and my dad made us chili dogs and homemade mac 'n' cheese for lunch.

The weather remained terrible. In fact, it started snowing. We had a White Christmas, which meant snowball fights and hot chocolate and roaring fires in the living room. It was fun for a while but after two more days of freezing temperatures, my sister started getting on my last nerve, and I was itching to get outside.

When the weather finally turned and the snow melted, Carlos and Dennis asked me to play soccer in the park. I realized I hadn't kicked a ball in almost a week. I don't think I've ever gone that long without playing!

I was eager to get back on the field, but at the same time, nervous about coming back too soon. So I gave my friends a lame excuse and hung out in my room all day. That didn't relieve my boredom, and Messi kept flaring his beard whenever I looked at him.

Finally, I flung up my hands. "What?"

But I knew what he was thinking. My lizard's sixth sense told him I was moping around the room to avoid my problems.

"What do you want from me?" I said. "I'm *injured*."

My lizard stood on his hind legs and glared at me. It made me laugh, but it also got me thinking. Even if my growing pains got better—and what if they didn't?—I knew I was going to be so out of shape that Samantha couldn't play me. I didn't want that to happen, but I wasn't sure what to do about it.

I remembered what her mother had told her: Focus on what you *can* do and not what you *can't*. That sounded like something my own mom would say.

Hmm. I couldn't run or play soccer to get in shape because that could set off my growing pains. And I didn't know much about exercising in general. The older teams at the academy had trainers who did, but I wasn't there right now.

But I knew someone who could help.

"Alright, Commander Messi, are you happy? I'm going to talk to my dad about how to stay in shape. He played football and knows about stuff like that."

I opened Messi's cage and waited, expecting my lizard to climb onto my arm and nuzzle me.

Instead, he pranced back and forth, arched his back, and flared his beard again.

Still angry?

What is it with this guy?

I gave him more food, let him out on the bed, and told him how handsome he was. Nothing seemed to satisfy him.

Annoyed, I lay on my back and put my hands behind my head, thinking about life and soccer and all kinds of things. I know Messi is just a lizard, but we have this weird bond. Of course, I know he didn't really *know* something else was wrong with me, but he could sense it with those superpowers animals have.

I lay there for a long time, not wanting to admit he was right.

But I knew in my heart he was.

There was something else going on.

Another problem I had to deal with.

Goran.

No way I was quitting the team this year. Not unless I absolutely had to. And when I returned from break, if I wanted a chance to play, I had to be in shape. That much was obvious.

But I also had to fight for my position.

I stood and let Messi walk up my arm. His beady eyes stared me down, his beard puffed out like a bagpipe. I said, "I've been feeling awful sorry for myself lately, haven't I?"

I swear he nodded a little bit.

At that moment, something inside me snapped. I was *done* feeling sorry for myself. And whining and complaining, too.

All my life, I'd been a fighter. The small, skinny kid who clawed his way to the top no matter the odds. What had changed since the London Dragons summer camp when I'd worked so hard to make the World Cup?

I'd let success go to my head. Just because I'd made it to the Youth Prem didn't mean I could stop learning and fighting. And lately, I'd been using my growing pains as an excuse not to deal with Goran.

When it came to that guy, my growing pains weren't the problem. He'd beaten me in the two v two challenge and shown me up other times as well.

I was the problem.

Goran intimidated me. He even scared me a little on the field.

There. I had admitted it to myself.

And now I was done with it.

I put Messi inside his cage and spoke to him as I paced my room. "Yeah, I know. I'm sick of it, too, and it's time to do something about it. When I get healthy, maybe I'll get my starting position back and maybe I won't. But I'm not going to roll over and let Goran take it from me. I'm going to fight him tooth and nail, Messi, just like you do in the jungle. I'm gonna give it everything I have and get better and get stronger and never back down again. From him or anyone else. Okay? Do you hear me?"

My jaw firmed, and I could feel adrenaline coursing through me, even though I wasn't playing in a game.

"It's on," I said.

I realized I wasn't tired anymore. I wanted to get started right this minute. As I left my room, right before I turned out the light, I noticed Messi's beard had finally relaxed.

⚽ ⚽ ⚽

I found my dad on the screen porch, warming his hands by the wood-burning stove.

"Hey, son. I'd love for you to join me but it's freezing tonight. Why don't you put on a jacket?"

"Yeah. Okay. In a second. I just wanted to know... I wanted to know if you could do something for me."

"Of course. What is it?"

I looked him in the eye. "I want you to train me."

ENTRY #21

The Dungeon Crawl

My dad leaned back in his chair. "You want me to do what?"

"Train me. Get me in shape. Make me stronger and tougher."

He took a sip from the cup he was holding. I thought he might laugh, but his face was calm and his eyes were bright with a sudden light. "I've noticed you haven't touched a soccer ball since you've been home. I assumed you were letting your legs heal."

"Yeah."

"So what's this about?"

I hesitated, then told him everything. About how my growing pains had led to my lack of playing time, and how Goran had taken my position and was a bigger, stronger player.

How I needed to get in shape and fight back.

It felt good to get it all off my chest. When I finished, my dad's strong jaw tightened, and he patted the chair next to him. "Why don't you go get a jacket, son. And let's talk."

⚽ ⚽ ⚽

That night, my new exercise routine began.

Under my dad's guidance, I did seventy-five pushups—five sets of fifteen, because that's all I could do at one time. I didn't cheat either, like I usually do. My dad made sure I went all the way down and kept my back straight. I also did fifty sit-ups (that took a while, too), fifty mountain climbers, and fifty burpees. That's an exercise my dad used to do on his football team and in the army. Let me tell you: Burpees are modern-day torture. About as much fun as crawling through green slime while eating rotten bananas.

After I finished with all that, I was so exhausted I went to bed and fell right asleep.

It snowed three inches overnight. In the morning, I did all the exercises again. None of them hurt my legs. I mean, they all made me sore, but not in the painful way that growing pains do.

Before lunch, I did another full set, huffing and puffing my way through. In the afternoon, my dad told me to go around the neighborhood, knock on doors, and shovel snow off the driveway of anyone who needed help. I did that for three hours, ate dinner, and did another round of exercises before bed.

Then I slept like a bear in hibernation.

Over the next two weeks, every day, my dad added more exercises and more chores. I chopped wood, organized boxes in the garage, and cleared out Aunt Janice's attic. In the backyard, my dad has a shed with weight training equipment. He and I did pullups together, triceps dips, and squats holding sacks of potatoes. We also did exercises called lunges, which are a terrible thing to do to someone, and wall walks, which are even worse—you have to do a pushup facing away from a wall, then kick your legs up on the wall and walk up it as high as you can. My stomach muscles burned with every rep.

For the rest of the week all I did was train and do chores.

Every type of exercise you can imagine that doesn't involve running. It felt like a dungeon crawl in real life. You know what I'm talking about? Those video games where you plow through level after level of hard-core dungeons infested with monsters? And it just gets harder the farther you go?

Same with this. Every time I made some gains, my dad increased the number of reps or made the chores harder or introduced a horrible new workout.

I've always said I hate exercising just for the sake of it, without a ball and goals and players trying to score.

That's still true. In fact, I hate exercise even more now than before.

But it was working. I got a little stronger every day. Two days before I had to return to London, I could do forty push-ups in a row, which is much better than I'd ever done.

Later that night, I stood in front of the mirror and flexed.

And saw a little improvement! My arms looked a tiny bit more defined, and my chest didn't look completely like an ironing board.

Something else: My legs hadn't hurt in days.

I swallowed, not wanting to jinx myself, then decided I would try playing soccer with my friends.

⚽ ⚽ ⚽

"About time, Leo," Carlos said as we gathered in the park the next morning with Dennis and eight more of our friends. The temperature was still freezing, but we were all desperate to play. "I hope you were sick and not actually doing chores and exercises like you've been telling us."

"Truth," I said.

"Huh? Did something happen to you? Maybe an alien took over your brain?"

I chuckled and started juggling. "We gonna play or what?"

"Sure," Dennis said. "All of us against you?"

"Don't give him a bigger head than he already has," Carlos said. "I'll pick teams."

"Don't worry," I said. "I'm taking it easy."

"I'm not worried. Why would I be?"

Dennis laughed, and light snow began to fall as Carlos kicked off to a teammate. I had made sure to warm up, and I wasn't going to run any full sprints or anything. Just a light pickup game with my friends. It was good to feel the ball again, and I smiled the first time I made a run, toasted two people, and flicked the ball through the cones for an easy goal. What a relief to be playing soccer instead of struggling through push-ups, pullups, and burpees.

"Okay," Dennis said after I scored my third goal in about two minutes. "New rules: Leo can't use his right foot, take more than three dribbles at a time, or pass to his left."

Everyone applauded that, and I solemnly promised to obey.

And still scored the next goal. By this time, everyone had rearranged the teams, so I was playing with three teammates against the other six players.

"Ridiculous," Carlos grumbled as we took a water break. "Leo isn't *that* good."

"Really?" Dennis said. "Is that why he just nutmegged you with *only his left foot* two times in a row? And told you he was going to do it?"

Carlos mumbled something under his breath.

I laughed and eased off for the rest of the game. We had a great time and played until our fingers and toes were numb from cold.

The best thing of all?

I didn't feel a single twitch of pain.

⚽ ⚽ ⚽

The next morning, after my strength training exercises, I decided to go on a mile run.

Still no pain.

Then I gulped down a glass of water and started packing for London, hardly daring to believe my legs weren't hurting, hoping against hope my growing pains were gone.

In the afternoon, Aunt Janice took me shopping for some clothes that fit better, and that night, my dad called me out to the screen porch. "Ready for the flight?" he asked.

"Yup."

"How are you feeling?"

"Good," I said.

"That's it? Not stronger, tougher, in better shape than you've ever been?"

I grinned. "Really good."

He patted me on the knee. "Glad to hear it. You look stronger, too."

"I do?"

"You bet. It takes time, son, and you can only do so much at your age. There's no reason to stress or worry. Just let nature take its course. Your body will grow how and when it wants. But you *can* improve on what nature gives you, and you're doing a great job of that. Keep it up. You'll see real improvement, I guarantee it."

"Thanks, Dad," I said. "You've helped a lot."

He got up and placed another log into the wood-burning stove. The fire roared and crackled inside. "Couple more things," he said.

"Yeah?"

"I've been hearing a lot about this Goran kid."

I looked off to the side.

"Back in my playing days," he said, "whenever I was in competition with someone bigger and stronger—"

"Wait." I glanced at his bulging arms beneath his coat. "There was someone bigger and stronger than you?"

"Son, there's *always* someone bigger and stronger. And faster, and smarter, and better. Anyway, you know what I did? I found someone even bigger and stronger than my competition, and I trained against them. Even if I had to seek out older boys. I did this on the JV team, and it helped me make varsity."

"Hmm. Okay."

"But size and strength are only part of the equation, especially in soccer. Are you quicker than this guy?"

"Definitely."

"More skilled?"

"I think so. We're very different players."

"Then use your talents. Play to *your* strengths."

I nodded. "Okay."

"And finally, Leo, to be honest, I don't want to hear about Goran anymore. Or anyone else. I want to hear about *you*. It's almost like you're training and playing to beat this one guy instead of doing it for yourself and the love of the game. Stop thinking that way. It will limit your horizons. You need to be the best version of yourself, no matter who you're playing against. Focus on *you*, not on Goran or anyone else. You hear me?"

"Yes, sir."

"Good. Now go finish packing and do your pushups."

ENTRY #22

The Sleepover

Since it's cheaper to fly during the week, I left on a Tuesday and arrived in London on a Wednesday. Practice didn't start until Monday, so I had plenty of free time and looked forward to hanging out with my friends.

I planned to keep up my exercises, but I needed to start using a ball every day, too—as long as my legs didn't hurt.

When I arrived at the Caravan, I flopped on my bed and started thinking about everything my dad had said.

Where could I find bigger, stronger players to play against?

I could check and see if any of the U16 or U18 players were around this weekend. But most people wouldn't arrive until Saturday or Sunday, and there was no guarantee of a pickup game.

But I knew someplace there was *always* a game, with incredible players of all ages.

I turned on my device and sent a message to John.

> Hey, r u around?

His response came quickly.

> Yeah, bruv! How's it?

> Good. Want to hang at the Cage and hit Nando's after?

> Course I do. Why u back so early?

> **Cheaper flight**

Right. Hang on a sec, I've got a better idea

> **Sure**

A better idea? I thought. *What's better than the Cage and Nando's?*

Soon after, John texted back.

My mum said you can stay through the weekend. C'mon, bruv, let's hang! We can play every day. You'ze comin' or not?

I thought about it for half a millisecond, and texted back.

> **B there soon.**

Meet you at the Cage.

I hadn't even unpacked from the flight, but who cares? I threw some clothes and gear into a duffel bag and got permission from Samantha to stay with John for four nights. She even walked me to the bus stop and told the driver to make sure I got off at the right place.

On the way to Elephant & Castle, the neighborhood where John lives, I sat on the upper deck of a big red bus and watched the city pass by, thinking that John was right: The only thing better than Nando's and the Cage was *four days* of Nando's and the Cage.

⚽ ⚽ ⚽

When the bus driver let me off, he gave me directions. It was only a two-block walk. I had a skip in my step, barely able to wait.

This section of London is much grittier than Lewisham. There aren't as many trees and the concrete underpasses are covered with grime and graffiti. But there are tons of shops and people, and I liked the energy that seemed to crackle in the air.

Soon I saw a familiar gravel path squeezing between two brick apartment buildings. Some of the windows in the buildings were smashed, and trash and broken bottles littered the sides of the path. I was a little nervous walking by myself, but I knew John lived here and did it all the time.

The path spilled into a little park surrounded by looming brick apartment buildings. Inside the park was a playground with a slab of concrete surrounded by a high chain-link fence. Inside the fence—the Cage—were two miniature soccer fields. Each had half-size goals and lines marked in faded white paint.

School hadn't started, so there were players of all ages and sizes and colors on the two fields. More people were chilling on the playground or lined up outside the fence, cheering on the players. Just like always, the talent was incredible, and I spotted a few academy players I recognized from our games. I knew that plenty of Premier League players had gotten their start in places just like this all over London.

"Bruv! You made it!"

I turned and saw my short, stocky friend strolling towards me. The weather was mild for January, about fifty degrees with a clear sky. Like me, John was wearing sweats, a hoodie, and turf shoes. I noticed he had dyed his inch-high dreadlocks a deep shade of red.

We exchanged a special handshake we liked to do, bumped

chests, and headed towards the Cage. "You can drop your bag by the gate," he said. "It'll be fine. I know everyone here."

"Okay."

John snapped his fingers on both hands. "The wait isn't too bad. Lemme grab someone to play with."

"Hey, John?"

"Bruv?"

One of the games inside the Cage had players about our age, but the other one had players a good bit older, ranging from fifteen to eighteen. "Let's run with the older group."

He cocked an eyebrow. "Feeling good today, innit?"

"Not really. I'm not even sure my legs will hold up. But I want to practice against bigger players."

"All right then. All right. Lemme see who can help."

I noticed that both fields were three v three today, plus the keepers. To my surprise, I saw another familiar face hanging out at a picnic table with some friends. As John waded through a crowd of older teens, searching for a third field player, I walked over to the picnic table, bent down, and said, "JoJo!" right in her ear.

She jumped about ten feet high, causing her friends to break out laughing, then turned towards me with her fists balled. When she saw who it was, her fists relaxed and she rolled her eyes. "Leo, wut are you doin' here? It's still break. And you best be careful, you almost got cocked in the noggin."

I put up my palms. "I'm here to play. What else? Want to join me and John?"

One of her friends sniggered and said, "He's cute, Jo. You should go."

JoJo whirled on her. "You got a death wish, Marla? Shut

that trap and sew it up." Then she flung a hand in my direction. "Lemme know when we're on."

"Sure. Oh, and we're playing with the older group."

JoJo stared at me, her lips curling slowly at the ends. "Good."

⚽ ⚽ ⚽

When John returned, he was walking with his arm around a player who resembled a supersized version of himself: broader shoulders, bigger chest and arms, a few inches taller. He even had similar dreadlocks. At first I thought they were brothers, but John introduced the new guy as his older cousin Baron.

"Can you play?" Baron rumbled in a deep voice, then gave me a fist bump that almost crushed my knuckles.

John laughed. "Don't you worry about my bruv. He's got moves for days."

"We'll see." Baron glanced at JoJo and frowned. "Jonnie, you sure about this keep? On the older field?"

JoJo got right in his face. "You're big but I'm thinking you're short on sense. Can *you* play? Or are those muscles only good in the gym?"

"Hey hey," Baron said, cracking a smile. "Let's go then."

Soon we took the field against the winners of the game with the older players. Our new opponents looked about seventeen. I swallowed as I walked out, fingering the lion's tooth necklace under my shirt. Two of the players had arms as big as my thighs. Maybe I'd made a mistake choosing this field. How could we compete? They might run all over us and knock us down like bowling pins. We'd be the laughingstock of the Cage.

These older players were good, too. During the game, I'd seen them doing all kinds of tricks. Remember, winning is important at the Cage, but so is style. If you want to earn respect, you have to show some serious skill.

"They're Nigerian," John said as we walked out. "Two of them are former academy players. The skinny guy's name is Chike. He's an influencer and won some mad coin at a national tricks contest."

"What's this, Baron?" Chike said. "Did you raid the nursery for this team?"

"They probably weigh more than you, mawga boy."

After a little more smack talk, the game began, and John kicked off to Baron. The big guy spun around Chike with surprisingly quick feet, using his arms to keep the smaller defender away, then barreled forward and blasted a shot on goal. Their keeper slapped it away and threw the ball downfield. I remembered how fast games were played in the Cage. Back and forth the ball went, end to end in the blink of an eye. I hadn't been running and struggled to keep up.

Chike got the ball in midfield as Baron stepped up to defend. As John's cousin pressed against the much smaller player, trying to bully him off the ball, Chike lifted the ball on the side of his foot and moved his leg back and forth, somehow holding the ball in place, dancing around Baron and teasing him. It was an incredible display of skill that had the crowd roaring.

Baron got sick of it and ran Chike over. There was no whistle because there are no referees in the Cage. No one calls fouls unless there's blood.

The other two players were about Tig's height. One of them

tackled Baron and came right at me. I backpedaled, doing my best to keep him in check, but he flicked the ball past me and ran onto it. I sprinted to get back, but he was too fast and held me off with his arm. I worked hard but he ran by me and blasted a shot past JoJo.

"Too easy," he said, patting me on the head as he ran back.

Baron muttered something about playing with children and kicked off to John. After hesitating, John tried to slip through two defenders. Chike stuck out a foot at the last moment, stripping him. As Chike took off, I dashed over and picked his pocket from behind.

I dribbled towards the goal. The same player who had just blown past me stepped up to defend. "John!" I cried, faking panic as the older player closed in. I started to pass to my left, where John was streaking forward, then rolled the ball back and pushed it to my right, a quick V move that earned me a step on my defender. Caught off guard, he tried to recover, but I surged forward. The third defender raced over but he was too late. I curved a shot into the top right corner, earning shouts and whistles from the crowd.

"Too easy," I taunted as I ran past the player I had smoked.

That barb just came out of me. I probably shouldn't have thrown it. In response, he shoved me hard in the chest. A few months ago, that shove might have sent me to the ground, but my core was so strong from exercising that I took one step back and shrugged it off.

"Hey," Baron said, glaring at the player who had shoved me. "None of that, now."

The player started to retort, then took one look at Baron and backed down.

We lost the game 3–2, but it took longer and was much closer than our opponents expected. John scored our second goal, and JoJo made some amazing saves. I could tell we had earned the respect of the other team and the crowd.

Half an hour later, we played again. This time our opponents were even older, including a Welsh guy wearing a rugby jersey who was about six foot three. He had pinkish skin, looked like an American football player, and played like one, too, running people over whenever he could. It was kind of scary, to be honest, but I stood my ground and took my licks. He knocked me to the pavement a few times and shouldered me off the ball so hard once I went flying into the chain-link fence.

We lost that game 3–1, and the one after that 3–0. As the day went on, it became clear that Baron's main contribution to our team was guarding the other team's biggest player and making sure no one messed with us. Everyone respected his size, if not his skill. Baron was a good player but nowhere near our level.

John and I scored a lot of goals, but our opponents were just too big and fast and skilled. We played seven games and didn't win a single one. I had bruises all over my body, plus every move and trick had to be quicker and more precise than usual. I toasted some people and drew *aahs* from the crowd, but I got toasted plenty as well.

We left the Cage when it was too dark to play, and I had a huge smile on my face.

I had tested myself against some of the best street players in London, all of them older and bigger.

And my growing pains had stayed at home.

After JoJo left with her friends, John turned to me. "Bruv," he said in a solemn voice. "It's time."

"Yes it is," I replied, just as serious.

We didn't need to say it out loud. Without another word, we walked straight to Nando's and gobbled down fries and chicken pieces smothered in spicy peri-peri sauce. It was even better than I remembered. After we finished, I licked my fingers, leaned back in my seat, and sighed with pleasure.

"So how's it, bruv? Legs feeling okay?"

He knew all about my growing pains. "So far," I said.

"Ouch," he said, wincing as he reached for his drink. There was a huge bruise on his arm. "That Welsh guy got me good."

"Me, too."

John laughed. "What a gorilla!"

I laughed with him, and we relived some of the moments from the games. On our way home, he said, "Back to the other field tomorrow? It'd be nice to win a game or two."

I shook my head. "Nope."

He cocked an eyebrow. "What gives?"

After hesitating—it's embarrassing to talk about your failures and weaknesses—I told him about Goran, the exercises my dad had given me, and his advice to play against bigger, stronger players. "I'm not like you," I said, flinging a hand towards his barrel chest. "You never get pushed around."

John stopped walking. "Are you mental? Who do you think I played against growing up? My cuz and all his mates!"

"Oh," I said. "So you got knocked around, too?"

"Like a pinball." He slung an arm around my shoulders, and we started walking again. "I get it though. Ace moves are one thing, but in the Prem, you gotta be tough as well. We're gonna train all weekend long, you and me. Maybe we'll even win a game."

"I'm guaranteeing at least one win. Or I'll pay for Nando's."

John burst out laughing. "Then why would I try at all, bruv?"

⚽ ⚽ ⚽

The elevator to John's apartment, or *flat* as he called it, was still broken. His family lived on the top floor of one of the grim apartment buildings surrounding the Cage. The hallway leading to their flat was long and dim and moldy, but inside, John's place was just as bright and cheerful as I remembered, and I caught the familiar aroma of lemon and warm spice as soon as I entered.

John had three younger brothers, a sister, and an older brother who had moved out. Everyone came to greet us, including his mother, a sturdy woman wearing sandals and a headscarf with the Jamaican flag on it.

"Leo!" she said. "So nice to see you again. I hear you're staying for a bit?"

"Yes, ma'am."

"Good." She rubbed her hands together. "You two are just in time. I need some things from the store."

After dropping my bag, John and I walked to the local Sainsbury's and returned with the groceries his mother wanted. She was making curry for dinner. Neither John nor I had any problem eating twice, but I wasn't sure I would like the meal. To my surprise, it was delicious. I guess I like anything spicy.

The flat only had two bedrooms, so John and I made beds

out of blankets and pillows on the living room floor. We stayed up late listening to music, catching up, and watching anime. In the morning, John did my exercise routine with me, and after breakfast we headed back to the Cage. We were some of the first players to arrive and didn't have to wait for a game.

Over the long weekend, John and I followed the same routine: morning exercise, soccer at the Cage all day, Nando's for a snack, chores at John's house, dinner, and chilling on his living room floor. Though I was exhausted every night, I had the best time, and his mother fed us so much food I thought I gained a few pounds. No wonder John was so big!

Something else: Because John and I didn't win many games against the older players, we had lots of time to juggle and practice our moves. It was fun because there was always a crowd of people and great hip-hop pumping out of speakers. John and I made up a routine that got fancier and fancier. We joked that if we needed money for Nando's, we should start juggling for loose change on a street corner.

Slowly but surely, I felt more comfortable against the older kids. We kept losing, but I became less intimidated with every game. It was humbling because I'd never lost that much in soccer. But after learning how to shield someone twice my size, and brace for a hard shoulder charge against an eighteen-year-old, I knew it was helping me improve. They didn't take it easy on us either, because no one wanted to lose and sit out.

On Sunday morning, JoJo showed up again, but John's cousin had other plans. As we walked around, searching for a new player, I saw a familiar face walking down the gravel path with a pair of cleats slung over his shoulder.

"Riley!" I said as he walked up. "What are you doing here?"

"Whatcha mean? Playing football."

"I mean . . . so you're back from Manchester?"

He spat on the ground. "I'm here and I ain't ever going back."

I wasn't sure how to respond to that. "Are you on the team again?"

"Nah," he mumbled. "Got two more weeks of probation. Then Samantha has to decide."

"I know she'll let you back. We need you."

"Course you do."

"How'd you know we were here?"

"Samantha told me. I wanted to practice but I ain't allowed on the fields at the Caravan yet."

"Good timing. You remember how to play?"

He snorted. "You better give your 'ead a wobble. I ain't forgot nuttin'."

John and JoJo were just as happy to see Riley as I was. Though we missed Baron's size, Riley was a fearsome opponent who never tired. We even won a game, though the competition wasn't quite as tough as before.

In the afternoon, after a close loss, the four of us ended up at a picnic table while we waited for our next game, taking a water break and eating mango slices John's mother had sent. I didn't want the weekend to end.

When it was our turn to play, we started towards the Cage, but John grabbed my arm. "Hey, bruv, look who's here."

"What? Who?"

I turned and saw four familiar faces walking through the

park towards the Cage: Diego, Aron, Charlie, and Sebastian. The entire Dragons front line, plus Charlie in the goal.

They dropped their bags near the playground and got in line to play on the younger field. I don't think they'd noticed us yet.

"Hey hey," John said. "We might wanna play a game on the other field."

"Yeah," I said, watching Diego take out a ball and start juggling. "Maybe we do."

ENTRY #23

Cage Fight

The four-person Dragons team won their first game, obliterating their opponents 3–0. Diego scored two goals, Aron added another, and Charlie blocked everything within a mile of the goal.

When it was our turn to play, and I walked into the Cage with my friends, Aron and Charlie exchanged a smirk.

"Leo, Leo, Leo," Charlie said, shaking his head. "Did you come for more punishment? What was the score of our last game? Five-one? Six? I lost count."

"This is the Cage," I said. "Not the Prem. Doesn't matter though. We're gonna beat you both places."

"You hear that, Diego? Leo thinks they've got a chance against us."

"I heard," Diego said quietly.

"Who's gonna guard us?" John taunted. "You've got three attackers out there."

Aron threw up his hands. "Let's play already."

The sun was much lower in the sky. Clouds had gathered. I blew on my hands to stay warm as JoJo and Charlie walked out to the goals. Someone in the crowd, probably another academy player, said, "Hey everyone, it's Knights versus Dragons out here."

This caused a bunch more people to gather outside the

fence where we were playing and start throwing barbs and roasts before the game even started. I didn't mind. It was all part of playing at the Cage.

One of the players from the team who had just lost kicked the ball in the air to start the game. Aron and I were the closest players. As the ball came down, he backed into me, trying to shield me off, but I fought through it and poked the ball to John. He put a wicked stepover on Sebastian, then burst to his right and gave me a sweet forward pass. I raced ahead. Diego hadn't come back on defense, so the only person I had to worry about was Charlie. The big Australian came rushing out of the goal, his huge arms spread wide.

I reached the ball first but had nowhere to go. Charlie was right on top of me. If this was a real game, I would have passed back to a teammate. But this was the Cage, and I decided to try a move.

Going on instinct, I put my left foot on the ball to stop its momentum, then, in one smooth motion, rainbowed the ball over my head and Charlie's.

The crowd gasped. I have to admit, it was one of my best rainbows ever. Even I didn't expect it to work that well. As the ball came down and bounced towards the goal, I ran around Charlie as he scrambled to get back. He even pulled my jersey, but it didn't matter. I dove forward, sliding on the pavement to toe-poke the ball into their goal.

"Did you see that!" one of the spectators cried. "That kid just rainbowed their keeper!"

As I passed by Charlie, I said, "How'd you like that sauce?"

He snarled and dug the ball out of the goal.

Riley and John and JoJo mobbed me in the middle of the

field. "Amazing, bruv," John said, then pointed at the side of my leg, which had a bloody strawberry from diving on the pavement. "You earned it."

"Charlie ain't gonna live that down *ever*," JoJo crowed.

"You better watch it," John added. "He's gonna have it out for you, Leo."

Riley cracked his knuckles. "If he tries something, I'll flatten him."

"I'm not worried," I said calmly.

On the next play, Diego went right at John. Normally Diego is a straightforward player. He uses his speed and height to overwhelm his opponents. But this time, he used a fancy Maradona turn to blow past John. It was impressive; Diego's long limbs kept the ball out of reach, and he spun as gracefully as a ballerina.

Riley stepped up next, charging towards the ball. Just before he arrived, Diego flicked the ball in the air, hopped over Riley's outstretched leg, landed, and fired a missile at the goal. The shot smashed through JoJo's gloves and into the net.

As the crowd cheered the awesome display of skill, Diego ran back with a finger in the air.

Riley slapped the ground, angry at himself. I could tell he was a little rusty.

"Ready?" John said as he toed the ball on the center line, about to kickoff.

I nodded. "Let's go."

He passed me the ball. Aron stepped up. I gave John a return pass and took off. Just before Aron closed in, John slipped a pass to me through the middle, a quick give-and-go behind the defender. I took one dribble and saw speedy Sebastian racing over to cut me off, his feet pounding the pavement. As he arrived, I pulled the ball back, causing him to hesitate, then pushed the ball through his legs. I collected the ball on the other side and fired a shot on goal.

"Not this time," Charlie said, slapping the ball away. He threw it out to Aron, who chest-trapped the ball, kneed his next touch over John's head, took another touch in midair with his thigh, and then, before the ball touched the ground, fired a hard volley towards the top right corner.

It was an incredible move, but JoJo dove and swatted the ball aside. "Gotta do better than that," she said, collecting the ball and rolling it to Riley.

After observing the field, Riley tried a long pass deep into the left corner. John sprinted forward, but Sebastian was faster by a hair. He spun once, twice, keeping the ball tight, then flicked a pass to Diego.

I closed him down, staying low and strong, wary of his moves. The tall striker passed to Sebastian, who was sprinting down the wing. John didn't stay with him, forcing Riley to slide over. Sebastian made the smart play and gave Aron a simple pass in the middle. I was sprinting back, but Aron got a shot off before I could arrive. His powerful kick bounced off the goalpost and fell right to Sebastian, who poked it through for an easy goal.

"Two-one," Aron called out. "I thought this was gonna be a challenge."

Riley and John met me at the center circle. "Sorry," Riley said, huffing and puffing. "I should've cut off that pass."

"Nah," John replied. "My bad. I didn't get back."

I gathered them close. "Listen up." After outlining a play I had in mind, the game restarted, and I kicked the ball back to JoJo. I followed my own pass, calling for the ball again. JoJo gave it right back as Riley and John moved downfield, leaving me alone with Diego, who was right on top of me.

Just like I wanted.

Diego pushed against my back with his body. He was much taller and heavier, but for the last four days, I'd been playing against players even bigger than he was. I lowered my center of gravity, used my arms to keep him off me, and spun to my left. Diego is an incredible player, one of the best in the Youth Prem, but defense isn't his thing. He tried to stay with me, but I kept the ball out of reach, shielded him off, and pulled away.

I had known Diego would press, and I wanted to isolate him. Now it was three v two. I didn't give the defense time to set up. I surged ahead, forcing Sebastian and Aron to choose who to guard. Instead of staying back and buying time, letting Diego recover, Sebastian charged right at me.

Big mistake.

As he rushed forward, I feinted left, pushed the ball right, then cut hard to the left again with the inside of my foot. Sebastian's gangly legs tried to keep up, but I turned him around so badly he slipped and fell. I kept going as the crowd roasted Sebastian hard.

Now it was three v one. Left with no choice, Aron came to take me on. I stepped over the ball, getting him to bite, then slipped a pass behind my legs to John, right in front of the goal. He charged forward and slammed it home.

"Yeah yeah!" John said, as Riley and I raced over to celebrate.

Tie game.

It was getting darker and darker, but the crowd was bigger than ever, eager to see which team would go home with bragging rights.

On the next play, Diego burst forward, kicking the ball past John. Riley raced over. After faking a pass to Aron, Diego tried to sneak down the end line with the ball.

This time, Riley was ready. He stuck out a leg, stripped the ball, and kicked it downfield. John trapped the ball, turned, and looked for me. I was racing forward, trying to lose Sebastian. John slipped a pass down the middle. With Sebastian on my heels, I didn't have time to try a move. "Go!" I cried, making a one-touch pass down the wing, hoping John would make a run.

And he did. As I curled to my right without the ball, trying to shake Sebastian, John sprinted forward, took one dribble, and crossed back to the middle.

The pass was off target, too far behind me. I hesitated and then tried a bicycle kick, figuring I had nothing to lose. Wary of landing on the hard pavement, I caught myself with my hands and didn't strike the ball cleanly. It sailed over the top of the Cage and into the crowd. I jogged back, embarrassed, as the fans roasted my attempt.

To be honest, it was kinda lame.

Even worse than the last one.

I needed to work on my bicycle kicks.

On the goal kick, Charlie gave the ball to Aron, who tried to dribble around John. But John shut him down and forced a pass to Sebastian that Riley intercepted.

Our turn. I whipped the ball to John and curled around

him, calling for an overlap. John tried, but Diego stuck out a long leg and stole the pass.

Back and forth it went. For the next few minutes, we all tried to win the game with style, using tricks and fancy moves, knowing the crowd would love it. They cheered every successful move and jeered every failed one.

But no one scored. As it got harder and harder to see, we buckled down and focused on winning. This was a grudge match, Knights versus Dragons.

"C'mon," Diego yelled, when Riley stripped the ball from Sebastian. "Get me the ball!"

John and I took it downfield, two v two. After I curled a sweet pass around Aron, John tried a one-touch shot on goal that Charlie dove and saved.

The Dragons took it the other way. Diego feinted left, getting Riley off balance, then took a powerful shot from ten yards out that I was sure would be a goal. But JoJo dove to the pavement and somehow slapped it aside, causing Diego to throw up his hands in frustration.

I ran down the ball in the corner. When I looked up, I saw John streaking forward, and chipped the ball high across the field. John misjudged the trap, and it bounced off his foot.

I realized what had happened when I tried to settle a long pass from Riley and could barely see the ball. It bounced off my foot, too.

"Should we stop?" Sebastian said. "It's really dark."

"We're not stopping!" Diego barked, as he dribbled straight at me. "Not until someone wins."

"Agreed," I said, then stuck out a foot and stripped the ball. I passed to John, but his shot sailed high.

The game got a little wild as we struggled to make passes and traps in the growing darkness. A ball hit Riley in the face, Aron and John collided in midfield, and when JoJo slung out a pass to me, I could barely see the ball until it was flying past. It got so bad we gave up passing and stuck to one v one moves. But everyone was exhausted, and no one could take on the other team by themselves.

"Hey!" an adult voice called out, causing us to stop playing. I looked over and saw a man in a brown uniform jangling a set of keys. "Game's over. I gotta lock up."

"Five minutes," John said. "We're almost done."

"Nope. It's dark out here. How do you even see the ball?"

"We have to finish!" Diego said. "It can't be a tie."

"Sorry, lads. Rules are rules. I waited longer than I should already."

The man walked into the Cage, held the door, and waved for everyone to leave. Left with no choice, John popped the ball up to his arms and started walking towards the gated entrance.

Diego snarled and waved a hand. "We'll finish this in the Prem."

ENTRY #24

Back in Action

After the game, John and I made one last visit to Nando's. Riley and JoJo went with us, and the four of us talked about how badly we wanted to beat the Dragons in the Prem. Just like last year, we would meet them in the last game of the season.

Would we be ready?

Would we still have a shot at the title?

José was the Dragons' playmaker and one of the most important players on their team. He had taken his game to another level. Could I do the same? Would I even be starting? Would my growing pains come back?

One day at a time, Leo.

I was sad to leave John's house. After Riley and I rode the bus home together, we parted ways in the lobby of our building.

"Hurry up and come back," I called out. "We need you."

Riley hunched his shoulders and didn't respond.

⚽ ⚽ ⚽

I set my alarm early the next morning so I could do my push-ups and sit-ups and other exercises. I had to splash cold water on my face to wake up, but I felt good when I finished.

When I showed up at the field for morning conditioning, Samantha came over to welcome me back. "How are you feeling?"

"Good," I said. "Really good. I'm ready to practice."

"I'm glad to hear that. Still, why don't you take it easy in the mornings? Walk around the field while the rest of us run? At least for this week?"

I hesitated, knowing I would get even more out of shape. But it was probably a good idea to ease my legs into the second half of the season. "Okay," I said.

She patted my arm, her eyes full of sympathy, then blew the whistle. "All right, everyone! Line up for Carolinas!"

⚽ ⚽ ⚽

That afternoon, before practice started, I took a deep breath as I walked onto the field and started juggling. My legs felt fine after four days of playing at the Cage, and that was a good sign. But full-on practices and scrimmages were another level.

"Gather around, everyone!" Samantha said. We all took a knee around her on the cold grass. Clouds filled the sky, and a January chill seeped into my bones. My breath exhaled in little white puffs.

"We had a good start to the season," she continued, "but we've got a lot of work to do if we want to challenge for the title. Coach Anderson is going to lead you through some drills, then we'll scrimmage to get back in the swing of things. Now let's get our blood pumping and stay warm."

I hopped to my feet, paired up with Brock, and began making wall passes through cones up and down the field. For the next hour and a half, we ran through a series of drills with Coach Anderson that got increasingly hard, adding defenders and more complicated passing patterns.

Next we did a shielding drill with the same partners. I

pressed my back into Brock's thick body, keeping one foot on the ball while he tried to disrupt my balance. I dug in deep, lowering my weight into my heels and pushing back as hard as I could. I heard him grunting as he worked to knock me off the ball.

"What happened, Yank? Usually you're a pushover in this drill."

I kept pressing, using my lowered arms for leverage.

When he finally got the ball—it took him a long time—he came over and squeezed my biceps. "You're getting a little muscle on those scarecrow arms."

I wasn't sure if that was a compliment or not.

During the water break, I stretched and stood on my toes to see how my calves and Achilles felt.

So far, so good.

On my way back to the field, Samantha wandered over. "I want to let you know I'm keeping you at right mid for now."

I swallowed my disappointment. "No problem. Wherever I need to help the team."

"I appreciate that. You and Marco work great together."

The scrimmage lasted two hours. Both coaches stopped the play a lot to discuss positioning and other details. I felt good, and Brock wasn't the only person who noticed I had gotten stronger.

"Good effort, Leo," Coach Anderson said after I held off a challenge from two second team players. "I like that toughness."

That was nice to hear. I'd been worried that Coach Anderson was another Coach Purcell, and I could never do anything right in his eyes.

It was also a compliment I wasn't used to getting. In the past, I had always avoided contact, trying to slither my way through defenders. I knew I'd never be as powerful as Brock or Goran, and that my moves and skills would always be my strength. But it felt good not to be such a pushover. My dad's exercises were working, and I vowed to keep them up.

Maybe not three times a day, though.

I had tricks to practice and video games to play.

Speaking of tricks, I stayed after practice to work on my bicycle kicks. It annoyed me that I'd missed one so badly earlier in the season and embarrassed myself again at the Cage. Patrick and Ajay stayed with me. They wanted to work on their crosses, so they sent balls to the middle that I tried to bicycle kick into the goal. We stayed until dark and went to dinner together.

⚽ ⚽ ⚽

The next morning, I lay in bed for a while, nervous about getting up, wondering if I would feel a twinge in my legs. Finally, I rose and walked around my room.

Still no pain.

I was sore and tired, of course. But in a normal way. I knew what growing pains felt like now, and so far, they were staying away.

In fact, things felt good all week. I took the weekend off—not even a pickup game or a juggling session—then showed up Monday morning for conditioning.

"You ready for this?" Samantha asked, as we all lined up for the first Carolina.

"I think so. I need to get in shape."

She nodded. "Okay then."

I ran all five Carolinas with the team, came in last place every time, and almost threw up my breakfast at the end.

But my legs felt fine.

I almost whooped out loud. It felt like a dream or a miracle. I had gotten so used to having constant pain that it didn't seem real to feel normal.

But I wasn't out of the woods yet.

Playing at the Cage, practicing, and running Carolinas were one thing.

A full-length game, giving maximum effort, was another.

I wouldn't have to wait long to see how I felt, because our first game after the break was on Sunday.

ENTRY #25

A Mysterious Power of the Universe

The game was away against Newcastle. They were eleventh in the table. We were still fourth. All games in the Prem are tough, but if we played well, we should beat them.

On Saturday morning, we left London on a team bus. The ride took almost six hours, which is the longest we had to travel all season. Newcastle is so far away it's almost in Scotland.

When we arrived, the temperature was below freezing, and the wind chill made it feel even colder. No one had any desire to leave the hotel before the game. Instead, we hung out in the lobby and went to bed early.

I was sharing a room with Brock. On Sunday morning, before the alarm went off, he shook me awake. "Yank, check this out."

I yawned and rubbed my eyes, half-asleep. "Huh? This better be good."

He walked to the window and pointed outside. Fat snowflakes were falling from the sky. I jumped out of bed, walked over for a better view, and saw a thick white layer covering the buildings and cars. "Think they'll cancel the game?"

He snorted. "For a little snow?"

"Um, this is a lot of snow."

"We play in anything except lightning in England. Should

play in that, too," he muttered. "A little electric shock never hurt anyone."

At breakfast, Samantha announced the same lineup we had used before the break: me at right mid, Ian in the goal, and Kenji at center back in place of Riley.

⚽ ⚽ ⚽

As we took the field before the game, I jogged in place to stay warm. The snow blew in our faces, making it hard to see. All of us had on beanies and gloves and two layers of clothing, except for Duncan, who was *still* playing in shorts and a T-shirt.

"How do you stand it?" I asked him during warmups. His cheeks were bright red, and snow sat on top of his head like a white ballcap.

He blinked. "What do you mean?"

"You're wearing shorts and a T-shirt. The rest of us are freezing."

"It's just a little snow. I love this weather."

Sometimes I wonder if Duncan was raised by mountain trolls.

When the whistle blew, I ran extra hard to get warm. Soon my adrenaline took over, the blood started flowing, and I didn't have time to think about how cold I was.

We started the game well, but Newcastle struck first. Emile slipped on the soaked grass when he tried to block the Newcastle winger's cross, and their striker rose over Kenji for a header. I could tell our opponents were more used to this weather. It rained a lot in London, but it rarely snowed.

With time running out in the half, we tied the game after

Otto found Dmitri on a breakaway. Our Russian striker outran his defender and smashed a shot into the top left corner.

I thought I had played well so far. Nothing spectacular, but I completed lots of passes, never lost the ball, and helped out on defense. A solid performance that earned praise from Samantha during halftime.

In the second half, it started snowing even harder. At times I couldn't see the out-of-bounds lines. I guess Brock was right because no one said a word about canceling the game.

Duncan seemed to thrive in the terrible conditions. They didn't seem to bother Goran either. He controlled the midfield as always, keeping possession and barking out orders. We never spoke to each other except to call for the ball.

With time running out, the game was still tied. Yes, the weather was bad, but we weren't playing to our potential. We only had a handful of shots the entire game.

In the last minute, Patrick saved us by heading in a corner kick from Marco. It was a sloppy header, not that hard and with too much arc, but the goalie slipped in the snow as he was backpedaling and just missed the ball.

We eked out a 2–1 win but had not looked very convincing. Samantha seemed to agree.

"A win is a win, Knights. I'll take it. I know we all struggled with the weather—well, everyone except Duncan—but we've got a *lot* to work on. I didn't love our shape in transition or the flow of our passing. Our next game is against Liverpool, so we'd better be ready."

⚽ ⚽ ⚽

On the long ride home, I hurt all over from tangling with the big Newcastle players and falling time after time on the cold wet field. I was out of shape compared to my teammates, and so tired I slumped in my seat and put on my headphones to zone out.

Yeah, I was a bit of a disaster.

But I had a little smile on my face for two reasons.

We had won the game—and I still didn't have any growing pains.

⚽ ⚽ ⚽

On Monday, after practice, Samantha asked me to see the team physio again.

"I think it's a good idea," she said. "I know you're feeling better, but it would be great to hear what he thinks. I want to make sure I'm not overplaying you."

"Okay," I said, nervous about a return visit. What if he told me to stop playing?

Soon after, I was in the physical therapy building again, this time sitting on a bench in a large room filled with exercise equipment. Three other youth players were working out on machines. After talking to a U18 player with a knee brace, Mr. Nunn walked over to me and consulted a clipboard. "How are we feeling, Mr. Leo?"

"Good."

I described how the growing pains seemed to have gone away. He set down his clipboard, asked me to walk around and perform some exercises, then probed my calves and Achilles.

"No pain?" he asked.

"None."

He pressed his lips together. "That's great. Really great. If the pain comes back, ease off again, and come see me if it's worse than before. Other than that, I think we're all set."

"All set? What do you mean? Am I . . . cured?"

He laughed. "What I mean is that nature has run her course for now. I'm sure you'll keep growing, but hopefully at a steadier pace that doesn't trigger your Sever's pain."

"So I can play and run as much as I want?"

"You sure can. As I said, just listen to your body."

I could hardly believe what I was hearing. I was so relieved I stood there like a zombie.

"Right then, Mr. Leo," he said, picking up his clipboard. "You're free to go."

⚽ ⚽ ⚽

I walked back to my room in a daze. It was almost like some mysterious power of the universe had taken away my superpowers—my leg muscles—and returned them just as randomly. All those fears and worries about my future were fading like a bad dream.

I had a chance to really help my team now. But time was running out. If I wanted to make an impact this season, I had to work double-time to get in shape.

ENTRY #26

Grinding

When I showed up to the next morning conditioning session, wrapped up tight in my Knights sweats and hoodie, I saw Riley standing on a corner of the practice field, blowing in his hands, ready for a Carolina.

A bunch of us ran over to tell him how glad we were to see him. All the attention embarrassed him. He mumbled something in his thick Manchester accent, gave me and Otto a playful shove, and pulled his hood lower.

When Samantha arrived, she welcomed Riley back, and we all clapped for him. He shuffled his feet and looked down, even more embarrassed. Not a word was said about why Samantha had let him back on the team. I just hoped he was here to stay.

⚽ ⚽ ⚽

On the first Carolina, I managed to come in ninth. That was better than I'd finished in a long time. To my surprise, Riley came in first or second every single time.

When I asked him how he had stayed in shape, he shrugged and said, "Couldn't play football. Didn't have nuttin' to do but run."

During practice, however, his touch wasn't the best. He missed a lot of traps and easy passes that he would have made earlier in the season. Though he never spoke up, he kept clenching his hands at his sides, so I could tell he was frustrated.

⚽ ⚽ ⚽

Later that night, after I finished my homework, I made a decision.

Instead of listening to music in my room or playing video games in the lounge with my friends, I threw on some warm clothes, grabbed a ball and a water bottle, and headed outside. One of the practice fields had lights that we could use whenever we wanted. I flicked on the timer, and the halogen lights atop the big wooden poles flickered to life. It was only eight o'clock, but it felt much later.

I shivered in the cold night air, and my breath exhaled in little white clouds. Beneath an umbrella of twinkling stars, I walked to one of the corner flags, toed the chalked line, and started running. I did a full lap around the field—one Carolina—as fast as I could. I didn't time myself or anything. I just pushed hard.

When it was finished, I stood there all alone by the corner flag, trying to catch my breath.

This was terrible.

I hated running without a ball.

What kind of a moron would do this to themselves?

But as soon as I recovered, I ran another one.

And another.

And another.

After the fifth one—the same amount we did every morning—I did shorter sprints across the field. Now huffing and puffing and sweating under my layers of clothing, I sat on a bench and drank some water. Then I took out my ball and started goofing around. Juggling, practicing tricks, taking shots on goal.

By the time I returned to my room, it was almost ten o'clock.

⚽ ⚽ ⚽

I was tired the next morning. But I forced myself to get up and push through my sit-ups, pushups, wall walks, and all the other exercises. It felt like grinding through a video game. You know what I mean? Spending all those long hours slaying monsters and searching for loot so you can unlock new levels and get to all the good stuff.

In the morning, I finished tenth on the first Carolina—worse than yesterday. That was disappointing. Was I doing too much? Tiring myself out? I grimaced and kept going.

Later that evening, I returned to the practice field and repeated the same routine from the night before. After the final Carolina, I collapsed on the ground, exhausted.

A voice called out right behind me. "Whatcha doin'?"

I jumped about ten feet high, whipped around, and saw Riley standing with a ball in his hands. I took out my earbuds and said, "Running."

"Yeah, duh, I can see that. Wut for?"

"To get back in shape. What are *you* doing here?"

He looked down at his ball. "Same thing, I guess. Thought I'd train a bit. Got behind, too."

I pushed to my feet and slapped the ball out of his hands. As his face twisted into a snarl, I flicked the ball in the air and started juggling. "So let's train," I said, passing him the ball with the top of my knee.

His snarl changed to a grin, and he passed it back.

⚽ ⚽ ⚽

On Saturday, we played Liverpool and tied them 0–0. Since there weren't any goals, I won't bore you with the details. It was kind of a lame game, to be honest. Both sides seemed afraid to take risks, as if worried about falling behind in the table.

But that wasn't smart, because the Dragons won their game against Brighton, so they moved even further ahead. Ouch. Now the Dragons had a five-point lead on Liverpool and Oxford, and a six-point advantage on us.

Samantha wasn't happy with our effort. It wasn't that any one player made a bunch of mistakes. Something just wasn't clicking.

After the game, I decided to take the rest of the weekend off. No late-night runs or morning exercises. I was exhausted and sore and didn't want to push too hard.

⚽ ⚽ ⚽

"Where you been, Yank?" Brock said on Sunday night as we gathered in his room to relax. Otto and Patrick and Ajay were there, too. "We barely saw you last week. In the lounge, I mean. You been studying with Ajay or something?"

"Nah," Patrick said. "That tricky wicky is probably practicing FIFA behind our backs. You've got a PlayStation in your room, don't you?"

"I've just been running. And practicing a bit."

Patrick looked stunned. "Running? On your own? Why would you do such a terrible thing?"

Otto threw a pillow at him. "So he can catch up," Otto said, then turned to me. "You're feeling better?"

They knew all about my growing pains. "Yeah," I said. "A lot."

"Good," Brock said. "Now get your position back so the *team* can start playing better."

I looked off to the side, knowing it wasn't that easy. There was a moment of uncomfortable silence. None of my friends had ever said anything about Goran playing center mid instead of me. At least not to my face.

Ajay was sitting on the floor with a textbook in his lap. "Maybe I'll go with you," he said quietly. "I could use the practice. With the ball, I mean. Not the running."

I shrugged. "Sure. Riley's been coming too."

"Riley?" Patrick said in disbelief. "Extra practice? Is the world ending?"

Otto rolled his eyes. "Do you pay attention to anything? Kenji took his position, and he's been playing great. Kenji, I mean. And Riley *hates* sitting on the bench."

"Huh," Patrick said, as if he'd never thought about it, then went back to watching YouTube videos.

I noticed the conversation had caused Ajay's cheeks to darken, and he buried his head deeper in his textbook.

⚽ ⚽ ⚽

On Monday, a blustery but mild winter day, my legs felt as fresh as mountain air. I came in third on the first Carolina, which caused Samantha's eyebrows to lift.

"Great pace, Leo."

My times slowly worsened after that, but I still finished in the top half instead of near the bottom. After the Carolinas, Coach Anderson surprised us by calling out three rounds of forty pushups and sit-ups. I surprised him by completing every single one.

As I left the field, ready for a hot shower before class, I felt eyes on my back. I turned and saw Goran staring right at me. I watched him for a second, unable to read his expression, then kept walking.

⚽ ⚽ ⚽

That night, Ajay and Riley met me on the practice field. So did Brock and Otto. No one ran Carolinas with me except Otto, who wanted to get in better shape, but we all kicked the ball around.

The night after that, Patrick and JoJo joined us, too.

"Glad you're here," I said to JoJo. "We need a keeper."

"Then you best get another one. Cuz I'm here to work on something else."

I blinked. "Like what?"

She fidgeted with the drawstring of her purple-and-black hoodie. "I was wondering if you could teach me how to dribble. And trap and pass, too. I mean, course I know the basics, but I want to get better." She shuffled her feet. "I know I can block shots better than Ian. He's got hands of stone, innit? But the managers . . . they want me to do all the other stuff, too."

"How about you keep for us half the time," I said, "and play in the field the rest?"

"Yeah," she said, though she looked as if she'd just swallowed a frog. "Sure."

As the week went on, everyone focused on something different during the night sessions. I practiced my bicycle kicks and other moves. I did so many bicycles that I spent more time on my back than on my feet. When it came to skills and tricks, it bugged me if I wasn't perfect.

Along with JoJo, Ajay and Brock and Riley also wanted to work on their touch. Otto and Patrick and I led them through some basic drills, coaching every detail. Then we played small-sided games with tiny goals. That's the best way to get better with your feet. Patrick, Otto, and I played against the other four, which made the games pretty even. We didn't run around that much because we were all tired from practice. Instead, we focused on foot skills and short quick passes.

JoJo was so bad it was funny. She couldn't dribble around anyone and could barely complete a pass under pressure. Riley roasted her so much that JoJo yanked on his rattail and threatened to leave. The rest of us had to calm her down and tell Riley to take it easy.

By the next week, the entire team knew some of us were practicing at night. But only three others joined us: Duncan, Kenji, and someone unexpected who walked onto the field on Wednesday night, just after I finished my last Carolina.

"Hey," Marco said in a calm voice as everyone stared at him. "Is there room for one more?"

"Uh, sure," I said. I looked behind him but saw no sign of Goran, Dmitri, Ian, or Emile. "We're about to play a game. You'll make four on four."

He gave a single nod. "Okay."

We shuffled teams around to make them even. I guarded JoJo but didn't play very hard, letting her work on her skills. Both Brock and Ajay had made improvements and were getting better at threading balls through tight spaces. At first, I worried Marco might have come to start trouble, but he was all business as usual.

When everyone decided to leave, I walked off the field with him. "See you tomorrow night?"

"Yeah. I'm trying to work on a few things."

"Like what?"

"Turning under pressure and using my left foot. How are you so good with both feet?"

"I'm not sure. I guess I've been practicing with them all my life."

"Do you play a lot? I mean, when you're not with the team?"

"Whenever I can," I said. "Don't you?"

"Almost never."

"What? But you're really good."

He looked off to the side. "I don't actually like playing that much. I mean, the games are fun, but I don't like practicing. Football isn't my . . . how do you say in English . . . it isn't my passion."

That stunned me. "Then why do you play for the Academy?"

He shrugged. "I guess because I *am* good. And it's a way to get where I want to go."

"Where's that?"

"I want to go to college in America and work for NASA. Most of all, I want to be an astronaut."

"Cool. Though what does that have to do with soccer?"

"If I don't make the Prem, I'll get a college scholarship to play. If I do make the Prem, I'll pay for school myself. My family isn't poor or anything. We have a coffee farm near Medellin. But top American schools are very expensive. Hey, keep all this between us, *sí*? I don't think the coaches need to hear about my future plans."

"No problem."

We walked in silence for a bit. Eventually, I said, "You know, I was surprised you came out tonight."

"Why?"

"I guess because you're always with the other guys. I didn't think you liked any of us."

"Who says I do?"

"Oh, I just thought—"

He laughed and smacked me on the arm. "That was a joke. At practice, you said anyone was welcome to come. And none of you have ever asked me to hang out. So I guess we both made assumptions."

I supposed he was right about that.

⚽ ⚽ ⚽

Over the next month, I kept grinding.

Pushups, sit-ups, morning runs, night sessions, practice, classes, homework, games on the weekend. Sometimes I took Saturday or Sunday off, but sometimes I went to the Cage on my free days to play against older players.

I barely had time to sleep, but I got stronger and stronger, and my growing pains stayed out of sight.

So far, we had played twenty-two games in the season. We

had eight to go, and our record was 15–4–3. Not bad for a team that finished next-to-last the year before.

Unfortunately, we were still six points behind the Dragons, hanging in there but not improving. I think the entire league was stronger this year because no one had come close to going undefeated.

As for me, I'd been playing better and better since the break. I finally felt like myself again.

Actually, no. I didn't feel like my old self.

I felt better.

⚽ ⚽ ⚽

On a drizzly Tuesday in March, I walked to the field early and toed the line near the corner flag, ready for the first Carolina. Samantha blew the whistle, and I churned my legs forward, keeping pace with Riley and Dmitri and Kenji, who always finished near the top. Near the end, I surged forward, overtaking all of them.

"First place, Leo," Samantha said as I returned to the corner flag and slapped it with my hand. "I'm impressed."

I finished in the top five every time. Otto's night training had also paid off. In the past, he faded hard by the fifth Carolina and usually came in at the bottom with Brock. This time, Otto came in ninth, a big improvement.

My other friends had leveled up, too. JoJo looked more comfortable with the ball at her feet, Ajay had learned a few moves, and Brock was getting better with quick passes under pressure. We had all been working hard, and I hoped it would pay off in the games.

And we had a big one coming up that weekend, against the Manchester Marauders. They were fifth in the table, just below us.

Samantha did make a change to start the game—but it wasn't one that any of us expected.

ENTRY #27

A Tale of Two Halves

Usually, Samantha reveals the starting lineup during the final practice of the week. Sometimes, however, she waits until the last minute.

"All right, everyone," she said in the dressing room before our home game against the Marauders. "Here's how we're lining up."

She moved aside, revealing a whiteboard with eleven names. I was still at right mid. The only change was in defense. Riley was starting at right center back, his old position, and Kenji had moved to the left.

Which meant Brock wasn't in the lineup.

I stared at the whiteboard in shock. Since Riley had returned, Samantha had used him as a substitute for Brock and Kenji. But Riley had been playing better and better, and I guess Samantha decided she couldn't keep him out of the starting lineup any longer.

But taking Brock out?

He was the heart and soul of our team. Yes, Kenji was a great player, but he wasn't as tough as Brock or as good a leader. Whenever our team energy was dragging, Brock would wave his arms and shout and bring everyone to life.

As we left the dressing room, Brock walked out with his jaw clenched. This was one of the few times I questioned

Samantha's judgment. I knew she was trying to find a way to improve the team.

But was this the best move?

I took my position on the field. The noon sun was high overhead. The last time we played the Marauders, we beat them by a goal in their own stadium, and I knew they wanted revenge.

Nuno, their star player, took the kickoff. He was a tall and wiry French forward who gave defenses all kinds of trouble. After passing to the right winger, Nuno sprinted downfield, and the Marauders surged forward. They worked the ball around and got it back to Nuno. He went straight at Kenji, darting forward with his lightning-quick first step. Kenji back-pedaled, trying to slow him down. Nuno turned this way and that, then tried a spin move. Kenji stuck in a foot at the last moment, knocking the ball aside, but Nuno had almost broken free.

Emile recovered the ball, took a smooth touch to his left, and passed to Otto. I wished I was playing in my normal position, so I could make a run with my friend, but I gritted my teeth and stayed on the right, waiting for my chance.

Goran and Otto completed a give-and-go. Otto sent the ball to Patrick, who tried to dribble between the two enormous center backs. One of them slide tackled him, knocking him off his feet, and the other defender crushed the ball upfield.

After twenty minutes, I had barely touched the ball. At last I received a pass from Duncan. I stutter-stepped to freeze my defender, then burst towards the line, searching for Marco. He wasn't open, so I pulled back and sent a long ball to Patrick. After settling the pass, Patrick found Goran in the center. He tried a thirty-yard shot that sailed over the goal.

On the next trip downfield, the Marauders got a breakaway. Their right winger burst past Emile and cut inside. Kenji stepped up, but the winger slipped a pass around him, trying to hit Nuno on the run.

Riley raced over. Ian was coming, too. He had left the goal, sensing Nuno would score if he reached the ball first.

The three of them collided in the penalty box. At first, I couldn't tell what happened, but then the ball shot out from beneath their tangled legs and trickled into the back of the net.

Nuno's dangerously quick feet had poked it through for a goal.

After that, neither side had a good chance until right before halftime, when Nuno scored again. This time he rose for a header in the penalty box, soaring over Kenji and Riley. Although Brock couldn't jump as high as either of them, he knew how to use his big body to hold people off.

Would Nuno have scored that goal if Brock was playing?

Same with the first goal. Sometimes a player helps a team in different ways than pure skill. Brock was one of those players. He made opposing forwards nervous and had a way of making the defense better that didn't show up in the statistics. During the first half, I barely heard anyone talking behind me. It was strange because I was used to Brock barking out orders and directing traffic.

At halftime, in the dressing room, Samantha paced back and forth in silence. Her face looked troubled, and I could guess what she was thinking. In the first game, we beat the

Marauders in their own stadium. Now, after all the changes in the team, we were losing 2–0 at halftime.

Beside her, Coach Anderson was standing with his arms crossed and his mouth set in a thin line. It was so quiet in the dressing room we could hear the tick of a clock on the wall.

At last Samantha stopped pacing. "I'm not sure what's going on out there," she said in a quiet voice. "We're not creating any chances, and we're not playing with any energy. It's not that anyone is playing poorly. The passing is tight. We've had plenty of possession. But in the moments that count, we just... lack passion. This is a critical time in the season, Knights. We don't have many games left. To compete for the title, you have to find something extra for the second half. I'm going to make a couple of changes, but if you want to leave here today with a win, all of you are going to have to reach deep inside and find the will to turn this game around."

She pressed her lips together and swept her gaze across the team. "Brock, I'm putting you in for Kenji. And Leo, I want you and Goran to switch positions."

⚽ ⚽ ⚽

As I stood on the field behind Dmitri, waiting for the second half to begin, I bounced on my toes, thrilled to be in my natural habitat. I glanced over at Goran and saw him staring straight ahead. He hadn't said a word to anyone since Samantha moved him to right mid.

The ref blew the whistle. Dmitri took the kickoff and passed to me. I sent a one-touch pass to Goran, hoping he would play his best and not hold a grudge.

Goran passed to Marco and ran past him, calling for the

ball. Marco returned the favor. After driving deep into the corner, Goran sent a nice cross to Patrick. So far so good. A defender intercepted the cross, but Goran worked hard to get back.

It wasn't long before Nuno tested us again. He received a pass with his back to Brock and tried to shield him off. But Brock ran through him and stole the ball. The ref raised his whistle to his lips but didn't call the foul.

"Move!" Brock roared as he sent a long pass into the heart of the Marauders territory.

A swarm of players, me included, waited for the ball to plunge from the sky. Otto came out on top, shielding a defender before chesting the ball to me.

I settled the pass but had no space to maneuver. Two defenders were right on top of me. Without thinking, I pulled the ball back, cut to the right, spun left, and hit Patrick down the wing.

As we all surged forward, Patrick crossed to Marco, who one-touched the ball to the middle. I was running on to the ball but so were both center backs. I arrived first but again had no place to go. The two huge defenders were about to sandwich me. But in the corner of my eye, I saw Dmitri waiting to make a run.

When I reached the ball, I put a foot on top of it and spun halfway so I could shield off the defenders. But that was only part of my plan. In the same motion, I stepped forward, pretending to pass to Otto, then used my heel to kick the ball behind me, leading Dmitri into a patch of open space in the penalty area.

After making the blind pass, I spun and saw Dmitri's long

thin frame darting forward like a javelin. The ball evaded the jabbing feet of the defenders by inches, and Dmitri launched a one-touch shot into the bottom right corner.

Goal!

It felt great to get the assist, but after a quick celebration, we hurried back to our positions. We were still behind.

"Let's go!" Samantha cried. "Keep the pressure on!"

The Marauders came right back at us, working the ball down the right before trying to overload the middle. Nuno took a shot from just outside the box, but Brock slid and blocked it. There was a scramble for the ball. Riley fought like a wolverine and somehow emerged with the ball at his feet. He did a nice V-turn to escape the pressure and passed to Duncan on his right. Two Marauders closed him down, forcing him back towards our goal. Duncan passed to Ian, who worked the ball over to Emile. Before the defense could chase him down, Emile sent a beautiful pass up the wing to Otto.

Now we were cooking.

Otto faked a pass to Goran, then dragged the ball forward, fooling his defender. I made a diagonal run, switching places with Patrick. That confused the defense. Otto passed to Patrick, who immediately poked the ball forward to me. But he left the pass a little short, allowing a defender to close me down.

I had two choices. I could pass back to Otto or Goran and lose our momentum, or I could try something tricky.

I'm not sure why I chose the harder play. Maybe because I was feeling good, or maybe because I knew that sometimes you have to take a chance.

I reached the ball a hair before the nearest defender. As I

closed in, I reared back with my right foot as if I was going to shoot. This caused the defender to lunge forward and try to block my shot. As he did, I rolled the ball back and, with the same foot, pushed it behind my left leg.

I saw the defender's eyes widen. He tried to spin in time to catch me, but I was already gone, darting towards the goal. But now I had a new problem: the Marauders goalie, a heavy-set player with a face full of freckles, racing out to close me down.

Dmitri made a run down the middle. I faked another pass—this time with my left foot—then pushed the ball forward again with the outside of the same foot. The keeper, perhaps remembering my assist to Dmitri, took the bait and went in the other direction.

I took one more dribble and blasted a shot into the open goal.

"Yank!" Brock roared as he raced across the field pumping his fists. Riley was right behind him.

Patrick shook his head and wagged a finger at me. "You're one tricky wicky, Leo."

Otto picked me up from behind, Duncan pounded my chest, and even Dmitri and Emile came over to congratulate me.

"C'mon," I said as we huddled up. "We can't stop here. Let's get another."

On my way back to my position, Marco ran up beside me and said, in his quiet way, "Very good, Leo. Very good."

Fifteen minutes to go. We were so energized I thought for sure we'd get another goal soon. And we had our chances. Goran hit the crossbar, Otto missed by inches, and Dmitri got carried away on a breakaway and dribbled straight into their goalie.

But that third goal stayed just out of reach. We couldn't afford to drop more points, and I desperately wanted to score.

After Emile got too fancy with his dribble, and their winger stripped the ball, I worried we would fall behind again. The winger cut hard towards the goal and ripped off a shot as if he was trying to take off Ian's head. Somehow our big goalie got a hand up, deflecting the ball to the middle—right where Nuno was waiting.

Uh-oh.

I cringed, thinking Nuno had an easy goal, but Brock slid halfway across the penalty box to challenge him. He didn't get the ball, but Nuno was forced to take a dribble. As he went to shoot again, Riley flew in from the other side with another slide tackle, again disrupting Nuno's rhythm.

But the French striker was very good. He evaded Riley's last-gasp attempt, stepped to his right, and fired off a shot across the goal, beyond Ian's reach and headed straight for the back of the net.

Except our defense still hadn't given up. With a wild cry, Duncan came out of nowhere and dove forward, just in time to deflect the ball with his chest right on the goal line. His body slammed into the goal post, and Ian grabbed the loose ball and punted it out. Nuno stood there in disbelief, unable to believe he hadn't scored.

I thought Duncan might be injured, but he popped up as if nothing had happened, then tucked in a piece of his shirt that had come loose.

Our defense had saved us, but try as we might, we still

couldn't get that third goal. With a minute left on the clock, I knew we might have to settle for a tie.

Samantha thought otherwise. "Go, Knights! Push! How bad do you want this?"

Her encouragement gave me energy. After Riley stopped a breakaway and passed to Brock, I ran all the way back, calling for the ball. "Here!"

Brock gave it up. "Go, Yank!"

I whipped around and surveyed the field. The Marauders had gotten back quickly, wary of the counterattack. I pressed hard anyway. I could tell their legs were tired. So were ours, but the home crowd was feeding us energy.

I passed ahead to Goran and kept running. A defender challenged him. Goran made the smart play and gave it back.

Time was almost up. How could we break down their defense? I didn't see a good opening. All my forwards were marked. We had to do something creative.

I started right but shifted left, deciding to run with Otto. We could almost read each other's minds on the field. When I sent him a pass and looped around him, he passed ahead into space, knowing where I'd be.

I collected the ball near the sideline, gave it back to Otto, then made a run into the middle. Without looking, Otto flicked the ball forward, right into my path.

A defender stepped up. I faked another pass to Otto and cut right, getting the defender off balance.

Everything was happening very fast. Players cutting, spinning, working to get open. I had to make a quick decision. No one was free yet, but in the chaos, I spied Patrick's defender playing a little off him. I locked eyes with Patrick for the briefest of moments and saw him poised to make a run behind his defender. He couldn't leave yet because he would be offside.

But I knew where he wanted to go.

I raised a hand—giving him another signal—took a dribble to my right to fool the defense, and then, without looking at Patrick, launched a hard curving pass deep into the penalty box.

At first, the pass looked as if it was sailing out of bounds on the left side of the goal. I sucked in a breath, wondering if Patrick and I were truly on the same page. But then a flying red-headed spear appeared out of nowhere, launching into the air behind the Marauders back line. Just before my pass cleared the goal line, Patrick's neck snapped forward, and his diving header slammed into the back of the net.

ENTRY #28

Two v Two Take Two

The final whistle blew.

As Patrick fired arrows at the sky, I raced across the field with Otto and Brock to celebrate the victory. Normally Samantha waits on the sideline until we're finished, but this time she came out and high-fived every single player.

After the handshake line, I collapsed on my back with my arms spread wide, exhausted but glowing from the second half comeback.

That win felt good.

⚽ ⚽ ⚽

For the next two games, Samantha kept me at center mid and Brock in the starting lineup with Riley. We won them both.

Goran seemed increasingly unhappy. Before each game, when Samantha announced the starting lineup, he would fold his arms and glare at the whiteboard. During practice, whenever we crossed paths, he brushed past me without a glance. Sometimes I caught him talking with Ian and Dmitri, staring at me like I was the enemy.

On the other hand, Kenji didn't seem to mind coming off the bench. He could use both feet like me and could play all four positions on defense. Whenever someone got tired, he was the first sub off the bench. And sometimes, when Emile was having a hard time with an opposing winger, Samantha replaced him with Kenji early in the game.

We were playing better and better and seemed to have our swagger back. I think Samantha realized that although keeping the ball is important, it isn't the only way to win. Sometimes the best teams work together in ways that are hard to explain. Take Brock, for instance. He isn't the fastest defender or the best ball handler. But when he and Riley are in the game—the Terror Twins—they just make us better.

⚽ ⚽ ⚽

On the first day of spring, a crisp and sunny Wednesday with the sweet smell of pollen stirring in the wind, we took a field trip to Buckingham Palace. That's where the British kings and queens stay while they're in London, and I guess all the princes and princesses and dukes and lords and whoever else is in the club.

I'm not impressed by royalty. It's not like they did anything to get the job. They were just born into it.

The palace is impressive, but the tour of the inside got boring after about five minutes. It's just room after room of fancy furniture and old paintings. I did like the changing of the guard. That takes place in the courtyard, when rows of guards in red and black uniforms with funny bearskin hats swap places with the new guards coming in. It's very formal and feels like something from the Middle Ages.

During the ceremony, Patrick took out a soccer ball and began juggling. He wasn't in the front row of tourists or anything. But when our teacher asked him to stop, Patrick lost control of his ball, and it rolled right into the line of marching guards.

Can you imagine?

Our teacher was horrified, but the rest of us found this pretty funny. We all held our breath, wondering if the royal guards would stop the ceremony and throw Patrick in the dungeon. But not a single guard changed his expression or stopped marching. When the ball rolled through their ranks, one of the guards booted it away without breaking stride.

After Patrick retrieved his ball with a sheepish expression, our teacher almost sent him home. He apologized over and over, claiming it was a mistake, and she let him stay.

Though you and I both know Patrick has very good ball control.

⚽ ⚽ ⚽

After lunch, we walked through St. James's Park, which is right next to the palace. That was more fun. The trees and flowers were in bloom, lots of people were out, and we had high tea in a café by a lake. You might be thinking high tea sounds boring. I would agree except for all the sweet cakes that are served with it. I ate so much my stomach started to hurt. I figured I deserved it after all those pushups.

In the afternoon, instead of returning to Lewisham, we had a short practice right there in the park, on a level patch of grass. Samantha and Coach Anderson and a manager met us with a bag of balls and cones. The practice was very light, just some passing and footwork drills. But at the end, Samantha decided to hold another two v two tournament.

"It's a beautiful day," she said. "Let's have some fun in the park. You can pick your partners this time, and the winners don't have to do morning conditioning tomorrow."

"Pick our own partners?" Goran said, with a confident smirk as he walked over to stand by Dmitri. "That isn't fair. At least for everyone else."

A huge hand clapped me on the shoulder. "All right, Yank. We're on this time."

I turned toward Brock and frowned. "Sorry, I need someone good."

His cheeks turned red. "What are you—"

I grinned. "I'm *kidding*. Let's win this thing."

We didn't use goalies this time around. Samantha didn't want us kicking the ball so hard that we accidentally hit someone in the park. She made the goals smaller, but the other rules were the same: three goals to win, no offside, and no throw-ins or corners.

As Brock and I walked out for our first game, the birds were chirping, and squirrels raced through the trees. It was a great day for soccer.

Our first game was against a pair of second teamers. We beat them easily, then faced off against Marco and Emile. That was a tough game, but we pulled it out in the end.

Otto and Patrick knocked off Duncan and Ajay, then Riley and Kenji, before falling to Goran and Dmitri in a close semifinal match.

In the end, as part of me had known all along, the final game came down to a grudge match.

Brock and I versus Goran and Dmitri.

As the four of us took the field, the air felt thick with tension. The other players lined up on both sides of the cones marking the sidelines, ready to cheer us on.

Brock cracked his knuckles. "I'll take Goran."

"Nope," I said, staring down my rival as Samantha walked out with the ball. "He's mine today."

Brock looked at me in surprise, then shrugged and stood in front of Dmitri.

Goran started laughing. "Did you hear that, Dmitri? Leo thinks he can guard me. Christmas is early this year."

"Just play," I said. "And stop running your mouth."

Samantha didn't hear the exchange. She walked onto the field to ref the game, made sure we were ready, then dropped the ball between me and Goran.

As he went for it, I realized I didn't really care who won. Okay, maybe I cared a little. But my growing pains were gone, and I had my starting position back. I had proved myself on the field in the Youth Prem, where it counts. And there were more important things in life than soccer. (Not many, but some.)

So if Goran and Dmitri managed to beat me and Brock in the park, the world would go on. I could handle it.

But I *wasn't* okay with this guy pushing me around.

Instead of challenging Goran for the drop ball, I let him take it, then kicked the ball hard against his leg. It bounced off to the side. We both dashed after it. As we ran, Goran reached back to hold me off with an arm. I slapped it away and burst ahead, beating him to the ball. He grabbed my shirt. I shrugged that off, too. When I reached the ball, I rolled it back with the bottom of my foot, hitting Brock on the run.

After my slick pass, Goran threw his shoulder into me,

knocking me down. I saw Samantha raise the whistle, but I bounced up and called for the ball. "Here!"

Brock held off Dmitri and chipped a pass downfield. Goran, thinking he had clobbered me, was caught by surprise when I jumped up and ran forward to collect Brock's pass. Goran tried to run me down, but it was too late. I reached the ball first and poked it through the cones.

On my way back, Goran tried to stare me down. I ignored him, ran to the sideline, and fist bumped Patrick and Otto.

The whistle blew. Dmitri and Goran passed back and forth, working the ball downfield. Dmitri tried to sprint past Brock, but Brock forced him towards the sideline, where he didn't have an angle on goal.

Dmitri whipped a pass to Goran, who trapped the ball with his instep in midair—a beautiful first touch. The ball settled at his feet. He turned his back and shielded me off. Nothing I could do about that, but I knew Goran didn't have the moves to blow by me.

I let him shift this way and that, trying to get free, but I never let him turn. I could tell it frustrated him. He started backing up, trying to bully me towards the goal, but I kept poking the ball away and pressing against his back, stopping his progress. Eventually Brock slid over and stole the ball.

As I ran forward, trying to start a breakaway, Goran hip-checked me so hard that I crashed to the ground. I bounced right up, but Samantha blew the whistle. "Goran," she said calmly, "if I see one more foul off the ball, you're going to run until it's dark."

He whipped around to face Coach Anderson. "But I was just—"

Coach Anderson held up an impatient hand, cutting him off. "You heard her. Play the ball, not the player."

With a snarl, Goran backed up, ready to defend the free kick. I took it, aiming for Brock's big square head right in front of the goal. My pass was on target, but Goran rose high to challenge Brock. The loose header fell to Dmitri, who took off downfield. I raced to cut him off. It was going to be close. Dmitri decided to try a long shot on the open goal. I slid across the grass and blocked it at the last moment.

Dmitri got the rebound. I hopped up to defend. He dribbled forward, bobbing and feinting, but I watched the ball carefully. When he made his move, trying to beat me with a long dribble, I turned and ran the ball down, arriving a step before him. I spun and used some fancy footwork to pass to Brock.

As Dmitri scrambled to keep up, I bolted downfield. "Behind you!"

Brock was dribbling forward, backing Goran up. When I arrived to help, Goran danced back and forth, trying to guard us both. The small goal made it difficult to shoot around him.

I drew level with Brock. He passed ahead, leading me towards the goal. Footsteps at my back. Dmitri was coming to help. I had to play the first touch.

As Goran slid over, I scooped the ball off the ground, giving Brock a one-touch pass at chest height. Goran worked hard to get back, but Brock lunged forward and headed the ball through the cones for our second goal.

Goran kicked one of the cones, causing Samantha to give him another warning. After retrieving the ball, he stormed to the center of the field, kicked off, and barked an order to Dmitri. "Back to me!"

Goran got the ball and came right at me, a vein pulsing in his thick neck. This time, I could tell he planned to run right through me. He took one dribble, then another, and tried to blow past me on my left, using his body to keep me away. Sweat brushed off his hairy arms as I fought hard and poked the ball to the side.

In the middle of the field, the ball took a wild bounce off a rock, causing Brock to swing and miss. Dmitri dashed in and kicked the ball through our cones, making it 2–1.

Brock scoffed. "Cheap goal."

Dmitri ran a hand across his spiky blond hair and didn't deny it.

No one scored for a bit. Goran grew more frustrated by the second, stomping around and waving his arms. He even got angry at Dmitri, which I had never seen before.

A loose ball rolled into midfield. Goran and I sprinted towards it and arrived at the same time. We both reared back, swung with all our might, and kicked the ball, trying to win the battle.

In the last game, Goran had almost snapped my leg in half on a similar play. This time, I was ready. I tightened my stomach muscles, which were much stronger from all those sit-ups and wall walks. Then I braced my arms and legs and swung through the ball with all my might. I didn't cause Goran to stumble or anything, but he didn't win the duel. We kicked the ball so hard at the same time that it barely moved.

Goran went for the ball again, but I was quicker and rolled it back. When he lunged forward, trying to steal it, I lifted the ball in the air with the side of my right foot, then flicked it forward and ran past him. All the players on the sidelines lost their minds. It was a cool trick I'd never used in a game.

Knowing he was beat, Goran gave me a hard push, but I kept my feet and kept driving towards the goal. Just before I took a shot, Dmitri threw his body to the ground, trying to intercept it. I calmly put a foot on the ball, letting him slide past, then poked the ball through the cones.

3–1. Game over.

ENTRY #29

Family Day

After scoring, I high-fived Brock but didn't celebrate any further. It was just a small-sided game in the park against my teammates. No need to rub the win in Goran's and Dmitri's noses.

Besides, the players cheering on the sidelines were doing that already.

Goran was facing his own goal, chest still heaving, his broad shoulders slumped in disbelief. After a long moment, he stomped off the field without looking at anyone. Samantha and Coach Anderson both frowned at his behavior.

As Brock and I headed towards the water jug, Dmitri walked over. I braced myself, ready for a confrontation, but the Russian striker offered us both a fist bump and said, "Good game."

I returned the gesture. "Yeah. You, too."

After grabbing a cup of water, Dmitri walked right past Goran without saying a word. An obvious diss. Dmitri threw an arm around Emile's shoulder, exchanged some words, and the two of them started laughing.

⚽ ⚽ ⚽

Four games left in the season.

We were on a roll but still in fourth place. Over the last few weeks, the top teams had all dropped points by tying a game. But we were still four points behind the Dragons, and three behind Liverpool and Oxford. Any of us could still end up in first place.

In two weeks, we would play Oxford FC at home, and the Dragons would travel to Liverpool. A big weekend.

And two weeks after that, for the last game of the season, the Dragons would visit our home stadium.

So our fate was not entirely in our hands. To have a shot at the title, we needed the Dragons to lose or tie again—and *then* we had to beat them.

A lot would be decided over the next month.

⚽ ⚽ ⚽

Our next game was against the Camden Cavaliers. We beat them 3–2, but Samantha was worried about how many goals the other teams were scoring. We hadn't had a clean sheet in a while.

There were no games the next weekend. I stayed at John's on Saturday night and played at the Cage both days. JoJo and Riley came with us. JoJo's footwork kept improving, and she saved some incredible shots against the older kids.

I kept up my morning exercises and went to night sessions with my friends three times a week. I wasn't running extra Carolinas anymore, because I was in very good shape and didn't want to overdo it. But I kept practicing my tricks and helping my friends.

Ajay was coming along, too. He was a fast learner and very determined when he put his mind to something. He'll never be a top one v one dribbler, but that doesn't mean he can't be a great player.

Our next game was a big one: A showdown with Oxford FC, who were tied for second with Liverpool.

If we lost, our chances of winning the title would be very slim.

The game was also Family Day, which happens once a year. Before the game, the families walk onto the field with the players, then join us in the cafeteria for a pizza party. This was a bittersweet time for me. Last year, I had enjoyed meeting my friends' parents but missed my own dad very much. And it had made me think of my mom.

⚽ ⚽ ⚽

We had a great week of practice. After the last drill on Friday, as everyone huddled around Samantha, she revealed the lineup for the game against the Royals. When I saw the names on the whiteboard, I immediately noticed a change.

JoJo was starting in the goal.

I wanted to whoop out loud but instead I glanced over and gave her a thumbs-up. She sneered in response, as if she was supposed to be starting all along, and a serious mistake had been corrected.

My guess was that Samantha wanted to see if we could stop some of the goals getting through. Though I'm sure Ian was disappointed, he didn't let it show.

But someone else did.

To everyone's shock, Goran stood and faced Coach Anderson. "You said if I came here, I'd be the center mid. Not stuck playing on the right."

Ever since Samantha had moved me back to the center, Goran hadn't tried to hide his anger. He never let it affect his play in the games, but at practice and in the cafeteria, he barely spoke to anyone, even his closest friends.

Coach Anderson looked as stunned as everyone else. Then his eyes flashed, his jaw tightened, and he stood up tall. "No, I said you would *probably* be starting in the middle. You're still one of the best players in the league, Goran. Leo's just ahead of you right now."

Goran snarled. "I should be in the middle."

"That's for me and Samantha to decide," Coach Anderson said coldly. "And I suggest, if you value your future on this team, that you sit down right this second."

In response, Goran kicked a ball in anger, then slung his bag over his shoulder and stormed off.

"Goran!" Samantha said sharply. "Where are you going?"

"To find another team."

"That is not a wise choice. We're all helping the team, even if we're not starting. You're an important part of our program. But if you walk away right now, you're jeopardizing your future."

Goran waved a hand. "I don't need your help. Or anyone's. Plenty of teams will take me."

"Coaches don't want to sign players who quit their teams in the middle of the season. Come back, Goran. Finish out the year. Don't abandon your teammates."

But he kept walking.

⚽ ⚽ ⚽

The next morning, at breakfast, there was still no sign of Goran. Dmitri said Goran's parents, who managed his soccer career, wanted him to quit the team if he wasn't playing center mid. They felt it would hurt his future. Otto said that happened sometimes, especially when agents were involved, but I still had trouble believing it.

As my friends and I were discussing the situation, Samantha entered the cafeteria and addressed the team.

"Good morning, everyone. Who's ready to play today?"

A loud cheer broke out.

"That's what I like to hear. And I know we're all excited about Family Day. But let's get our heads straight for the game. We'll have time to be with our loved ones afterwards. Now listen." She pressed her lips together and put her palms on the podium. "I need to tell you that Goran won't be with us today."

We all exchanged glances.

"He's not leaving the team, but he refuses to play right mid, so we suspended him. He won't be dressing out with us either. I wish this hadn't happened, but we have to move forward. And we have to do that, Knights, as a *team*. We have to be of one mind on the pitch and off. A *family*. There are some of you today who won't have family members visiting, for various reasons. But you won't be alone. Look around you. Your football brothers and sisters are right here. We're a family, too, and we take care of each other. Got it?"

An even louder cheer broke out, and I felt better about not having anyone from back home at the game.

She nodded and ran her eyes across the room. "Good. Now,

since Goran isn't with us, we're putting Ajay at right mid. He's worked hard and deserves the chance."

"Ajay!" Brock roared, reaching over to slap him on the back.

The rest of us congratulated our friend while Samantha smiled. Ajay turned bright red, stunned by the announcement and all the attention.

"We can win this game today," Samantha said. "But we have to do it as a team. As a *family*."

⚽ ⚽ ⚽

The game started at one p.m. As we left the dressing room and emerged from the tunnel, I squinted in the sun and saw all the dads, moms, and siblings ready to walk out with us before the game.

It was interesting to see what everyone's parents looked like. Sometimes, like Brock's family, they looked exactly as I'd pictured them (large, red-faced, loud). Ajay's parents were both skinny and wore glasses and fussed over his collar as he came out. An enormous man with a wide forehead and owlish eyes gave Otto a hug, and anyone could tell that was his dad. Duncan also resembled a smaller version of his father, though it was obvious he got his shy smile and ghost-white complexion from his mother.

There was no sign of Dmitri's father, but his mother was tall and attractive and dressed in fashionable clothing. As she fell into step beside him, she reached up to pinch his cheeks. He tried to pull away, but she kept pinching and gave him a stern lecture in Russian.

But not everyone's parents matched my assumptions.

Take Patrick, for example. His dad was dressed in a business suit and had a permanent scowl. About the only thing they shared in common was their bright red hair.

And Kenji's parents, unlike their stylish son, dressed in very plain clothing. They didn't speak any English, and they walked quietly arm-in-arm with Kenji towards the stadium.

But the parents who surprised me the most were Emile's. He was so flashy and sophisticated that I expected a pair of movie stars to show up. But his mom and dad were both dressed in stuffy business clothing, like a lawyer or a banker might wear. They walked on either side of their son, and I noticed Emile's cocky swagger had disappeared. He was looking at the ground and even talked differently, without his usual slang. I mean, we all talk differently around our parents, but I got the impression Emile had a very different life away from the Academy than he had led us to believe. Instead of flying around the world going to fancy parties, I was guessing he studied a lot and did his chores.

Four of us didn't have any family members at the game: Riley, JoJo, Marco, and me. Marco's parents lived very far away, and I knew Riley didn't have a good relationship with his parents. But I was hoping someone would show up to watch JoJo. She lived in London, after all. When I glanced at her, she had even more of a sneer than usual.

As I walked forward, trying not to feel sad and homesick, someone stepped into view on my left, from beside the entrance to the tunnel.

"Hey, kiddo."

I turned in disbelief at the sound of my dad's deep voice. But there he was, standing with his big arms crossed and a smile on his sunburnt face. "Dad!" I cried as he joined me in line. "Why didn't you tell me?"

"I wasn't sure I could come until last week. Then it was so late that, well, I thought it would be nice to surprise you. Ginny and your aunt wanted to come, too, but tickets are real expensive."

I couldn't stop blinking. "I can't believe you're here."

"Me either." He took in the stadium and all the fans. "This is a little bit different from the YMCA League, huh?"

"Just a little."

He slung an arm around my shoulder. "Your mom would be so proud. Now what's your team name again? The Ninky-Nonks?"

I rolled my eyes. "The *Knights*."

"Just kidding." He glanced at the field again and began to slowly nod. "Well alright then, son. I guess you've landed in the big time. So let's see you play some soccer."

ENTRY #30

Knights versus Royals

The Oxford Royals were a surprise team this year. Unlike the Dragons and Liverpool, they're not a traditional superpower, and don't have the most talented players. They rely on defense to win games and use a 5-3-2, a very defensive formation.

No team has scored more than three goals on the Royals all season.

It would be tough to break them down.

Were we up to the challenge?

When the whistle blew, I passed to Ajay to help ease him into the game. His first touch was too heavy, and the ball got away from him. He managed to run it down, thin limbs flying, but it was a close call. I understood. It's hard to relax when you haven't started in a long time.

After a few more passes in midfield, I held the ball and surveyed the field like a war general. Keeping possession isn't an issue with the Royals. They have no problem letting other teams pass and dribble around the field, as long as they do it outside the penalty box.

I decided to try a long pass to Patrick. As soon as he received the ball, two defenders swarmed him. Patrick was forced to whip the ball back to Otto, who gave it to me. I tried the other side. But as soon as Marco touched the ball, another pair of Royals blocked his path to goal.

Finally, I tried a thirty-yard shot to test their keeper. He smacked it down and punted the ball to their right winger. He crossed to the middle, where one of the strikers got a step on Brock and blasted a shot on goal, top right corner.

Smack!

JoJo dove and knocked it away.

After Riley recovered the loose ball, he passed to Emile, who feinted left and used a rabona with his right foot to get the ball to Otto. Slick pass. I made a run, calling for the ball. Otto gave it up, and I gave it right back, a quick one-two that put him in shooting range. His right leg swung back and cannoned a shot on goal. It was on target, bottom left corner, but their goalie dove, stretched wide, and brushed it aside.

Not only were the Royals defenders hard to break down, but their goalie, a tall Saudi Arabian kid with lanky arms, was one of the best in the league.

Corner kick.

Patrick whipped a ball into the middle. *Splat!* Brock made contact with his big head, but the ball popped high. Dmitri headed it next, and the ball sailed backwards, out of the penalty box.

Marco ran it down. After one bounce, he tried a wicked half-volley that hit the crossbar and careened upfield.

The counterattack was on. The two Royals strikers passed back and forth, weaving downfield as Duncan scrambled to defend. He was our only player back, though Riley was sprinting hard to help out. Emile, like Brock, had been caught upfield.

Duncan worked hard to contain the two strikers. He darted this way and that, turning quickly on his stubby legs.

But two good attackers should always beat one defender. After a smooth final pass, the Royals striker on the right broke free and took a shot on goal from ten yards away. Incredibly, Riley almost blocked it. He had sprinted all the way back and slid halfway across the penalty box. But he arrived too late, and the shot screamed towards the top left corner.

JoJo had come off her line, sneaking out to cut off the angle. I thought for sure the Royals had scored, because the shot flew past her at close range and high speed. But she contorted her body like a gymnast, arcing backwards as she launched off her right foot and soared into the air. Her hand reached the ball just before it crossed the goal line, enough to tip it into the crossbar and back out.

The ball was loose in the middle. Riley was still on the ground. So was JoJo. The other Royals striker darted forward, ready to smack the ball into the open goal, but Duncan crashed into him, throwing him aside with a shoulder charge and clearing the ball.

The referee raised his whistle. I held my breath.

Would it be a penalty kick?

But the linesman kept his flag down, and the ref crossed his hands, the signal to play on.

"Great save!" I yelled to JoJo.

Ajay got the ball. When a defender closed in, Ajay spun to his left and evaded him, a smooth turn he never would have pulled off earlier in the season. He passed to me, and I gave it right back, using his speed to move the ball downfield.

Last season, Ajay played all over the place. Nothing seemed to stick, and Marco had taken his spot. But all that moving around had made Ajay a more complete player. He wasn't as skilled as me or Otto, but Ajay had put in a lot of work and wow, he could run. All game long, his speed and stamina stood out. He always got back to help on defense, then turned around and supported Marco on the wing.

As the first half drew to a close, we made one final push. Brock had just stripped the ball from a striker. We had a chance for a breakaway.

He sent me a pass in the middle, but a midfielder was on my back. I flicked the ball left and rolled right, slipping around him. The crowd roared in approval.

Another defender stepped up. I curved a pass around him and hit Dmitri on the run. He took one dribble but ran into a center back.

Patrick had slipped inside to make a run on Dmitri's left. *C'mon, Dmitri,* I thought. *Look up and give him the ball.*

And he did. Patrick received the pass in a great position, just inside the box . . . but another defender was in his way. Those guys were everywhere.

In my gut, I knew the way to score on the Royals was using runs and quick passes to confuse them. Patrick had the same idea, because he rolled the ball to Otto with the bottom of his foot, keeping it moving. Otto one-touched to me. I stepped up and let the ball go through my legs to Ajay, fooling a defender. We were moving fast now, getting the defense out of their comfort zone.

Ajay slipped the ball out wide to Marco. I curled to my right to support him. Marco passed to me. I stepped over the ball with my right foot, pretending to switch directions. Both the defender in front of me and the one guarding Marco fell for my feint. As they shifted, I cut hard to my right with the outside of my foot, then sent a little chip pass towards the end line, just past the defender guarding Marco.

Our Colombian winger took two quick steps, smooth and ruthless as always, and smacked a volley straight down the middle, right past the keeper.

1–0!

After the goal, the halftime whistle blew, and we celebrated all the way to the locker room.

⚽ ⚽ ⚽

"Great job out there," Samantha said as we grabbed our water bottles and sat on the benches, recovering from the first half. "That was a beautiful combination at the end. But a one-goal lead isn't safe. We have to keep pushing. Now listen, they'll have to take some chances in the second half. That should open the game up."

She made a few adjustments, such as moving Emile higher up the field, almost as another midfielder. Maybe that would get our offense going.

Before we left the dressing room, I heard her compliment Ajay on his play. He beamed in response.

"Let's keep the pressure on," Otto said as we took the field again. "Get a quick goal."

I nodded. "Let's do it."

Samantha had been right. Once the second half started, the Royals wingbacks pushed higher up the field, trying to stretch us. That gave them more attacking power, but it did the same for us. Not long after the half started, Ajay stole a pass and whipped the ball to me. We had numbers. I didn't see an easy pass, so I dribbled forward, forcing a defender to commit. Once he did, I passed to Otto, who sent the ball to Patrick.

"Kee-yaii!" Patrick yelled, flying down the wing. Deeper and deeper he went before crossing the ball right at the end line. Marco rose high and headed the ball back to me. I took one touch and slammed the ball on goal.

Whack!

The ball hit the crossbar, and I groaned.

So close!

The Royals had the next chance, but JoJo made another great save. Her pass to Emile wasn't the best, but he did some fancy footwork and kept possession. Again we pressed upfield. This time Dmitri got open. A defender stuck out a leg and deflected his shot just in time.

We were outplaying them but couldn't get another goal. Their goalie blocked shot after shot, and we kept hitting the crossbar or missing the goal by inches. You've had games like that, right? Where no matter what you do, the ball just won't go in the net? Like it's cursed or something? Or there's a forcefield in front of the goal?

Time was running out. I was growing more nervous by the second. The Royals started playing better and attacking harder, pressuring our defense. If they managed a last-minute goal, they would tie the game, and our title hopes would be ruined.

Riley made a great slide tackle on one of their strikers, but a wingback swooped in to steal it back. The Royals made a few passes before Brock cleared it away.

Our turn.

Otto and I ran forward, leading each other downfield. I

tried a long chip to Marco. His first touch was beautiful, chesting it down to his left foot. But his shot skipped off the ground, deflected off the goalie's arm, hit a defender in the leg, bounced off the side of the goal, and finally rolled out of bounds.

Seriously? The ball just wouldn't go in.

With less than a minute to go, we packed the box for a corner kick. The cross swung in, but the Royals goalie ran out and punched it away.

Their counterattack was on. It might be the last play of the game. I was bone tired but I summoned all my energy and sprinted back to help. We couldn't let them tie the game.

Their center mid advanced the ball quickly to a striker. He hesitated, then kicked the ball down the sideline. Their wingback beat Emile in a footrace.

Oh no. Now the Royals have numbers. The play had moved so fast that only Riley and Duncan were back on defense, facing off against four attackers.

Instead of crossing, the wingback cut the ball back on the ground. The right striker one-touched it to the left striker, who put the ball on a silver platter for the opposite winger racing inside. Time seemed to slow. The winger was deep inside the penalty box with a clear shot on goal. I felt the blood drain from my face as he stepped into the ball, striking a hard low shot to JoJo's left. The ball screamed towards the side netting. I didn't think she had a chance to save it, and I was sure they had tied the score, but for the second time in the game, JoJo shocked everyone by throwing herself to the ground as fast as a thunderclap, stretching out her arms, and brushing the ball aside with millimeters to spare.

ENTRY #31

Splinters and Hairs on Fire

After JoJo's save, the ball stayed in bounds. A Royals striker sprinted to reach it. JoJo scrambled across the ground and dove on the ball in the nick of time, then hugged it tight to her body.

Seconds later, the final whistle blew.

We had eked out the victory.

Brock started to pick up JoJo in celebration, caught her look of warning, and settled for a high-five. The rest of us danced around her as the crowd cheered our victory.

JoJo might have made a few sketchy passes during the game, but who cares? She had saved shots when it mattered most.

In the dressing room, Samantha announced some more good news: The Dragons and Liverpool had tied their match, which meant our title hopes were still alive. Not only that, but we were in second place, ahead of Liverpool on goal differential.

If we won our next game against the twelfth place Archers, we'd be playing the Dragons for the title in the last game of the season.

⚽ ⚽ ⚽

Later that day, all the parents and players gathered in the cafeteria for a pizza party. I still couldn't believe my dad was there. It was strange to see him around all my friends, as if two separate worlds had collided.

I invited JoJo and Riley to sit with us. Marco, the other player without any family, was at a table with Emile and Dmitri.

My dad and Riley couldn't understand a word each other said, which was hilarious, because they kept talking anyway.

"Leo and I had a good chinwag at Nando's," Riley said, describing a trip to the Cage for my dad. A chinwag means *having a chat* in British.

My dad's eyebrows knitted together. "A chin-what?"

Riley blinked. "Wut?"

"I'm sorry," my dad said. "I don't understand."

"Understand wut?"

"Did you say a chin bag?"

"*Wut?*"

JoJo and I looked at each other and burst out laughing.

Later in the party, my dad talked to Brock's parents for a while, as well as Otto's and Emile's. For the first time since I'd known Emile, his cell phone was nowhere in sight off the field.

Riley didn't seem bothered that his family wasn't around. In fact, he talked more than usual and ate more pizza than anyone.

JoJo, on the other hand, grew quieter and quieter as the evening went on. By the end, she was sitting alone in a corner, hunched over her phone. A few of us tried to talk to her but she snarled and said she was busy. After the party, she left with Samantha, who was probably walking her to a bus stop.

On their way out, I saw Samantha throw an arm around JoJo's shoulder and say something that caused JoJo to bite her lip and look away.

⚽ ⚽ ⚽

My dad had to leave in the morning. I wished he could stay longer, and see more games, but he had to return to work.

After breakfast, I walked him to the bus stop and made sure he knew how to get to the airport.

He chuckled. "I'll be fine, kiddo. I got here, remember?"

"Just checking."

He glanced around at the busy streets and tall buildings. "It's a little bigger than Middleton, huh?"

"Yeah."

"You watch your back, okay?"

"Yep."

He was still looking away from me. I noticed the side of his jaw working back and forth, and he turned to face me. "I like your teammates."

"Thanks."

"Where did you say that Riley guy is from? Mars?"

"Manchester."

"He eats even more than you do. How do they afford to feed you all?"

"I don't know."

He squinted into the morning sun. "I really wish I could stay, kiddo."

"I know."

"I'm glad you got your position back. Most of all, I'm proud you fought for it. Good luck in the last two games."

"Thanks."

He looked me in the eye. "It's been a tough year for you. I can tell you're stronger now. Both mentally and physically."

I nodded.

"All right, then." He gave me a hug and pulled away, leaving his hands on my shoulders. "I'll see you in less than a month. Beat those Dragons. Oh, and Leo?"

"Yeah?"

"You were great out there."

⚽ ⚽ ⚽

We had a good week of practice and crushed the Shoreditch Archers 4–0 on Saturday. Goran returned to the team dressed to play, but he sat on the bench and didn't talk to anyone. I wasn't sure if he was still suspended or had refused to play. Or maybe Samantha just wanted to use Ajay.

For the second game in a row, JoJo made some big stops, and when the starting lineup for the final game was announced on Monday morning, she was included.

Ajay kept his place as well. After Goran's outburst, just when I thought our team was in trouble, we seemed to come together. Our chemistry on the field was far better. Everyone seemed to enjoy playing together. Dmitri, Emile, and Ian started hanging out with the rest of us after practice and in the cafeteria. Ian even complimented JoJo on how well she was playing. It turns out he wasn't such a jerk after all.

I guess removing Goran from the starting lineup was like plucking a splinter from a finger. As soon as it was gone, the pain went away, and the flesh drew together. Maybe *that* was why Samantha was keeping him on the bench.

Though Emile had returned to acting like a celebrity after his parents left, we all knew the truth and teased him about his behavior when they were around. He laughed it off, but now he didn't seem so different from the rest of us.

As positive as we all felt about our team, we knew we had a super tough mountain to climb. The Dragons were the returning champs, the first-place team this season, and stuffed with top players. They had the two leading scorers in the league—Aron and Diego—two incredible center backs, one of the best youth goalies in the world, and a midfield led by José, who was even better than last year.

I grew nervous just thinking about the game. This time we were playing for a title, and the pressure would be on.

And, unlike last year, when we had taken them by surprise, the Dragons wouldn't underestimate us. They would be ready to play—and eager for revenge.

⚽ ⚽ ⚽

On Friday night, the players met in the lounge after dinner. Everyone except JoJo, Duncan, Ajay, and Goran were there. JoJo lived at home, Ajay was studying, Duncan had gone to bed early, and Goran was keeping to himself.

We were supposed to be relaxing before the big game tomorrow, playing video games and listening to music and roasting each other. And we did all of those things. But eventually, someone brought up the game.

"Yank, I hope you play this well against the Dragons," Brock said in disgust, tossing his air hockey disc on the table. Patrick and I had just demolished Brock and Riley in a game of two v two.

"Don't worry," Emile said, flashing a confident smile as he texted on his phone. "We're gonna crush them."

"I wouldn't be overconfident," Otto warned.

Marco spread his hands. "Emile? Overconfident? What are you talking about?"

This caused us all to laugh, and surprised me because Marco never cracked jokes. Emile put up a hand, as if to say, *Whatever, dude.*

"According to statistics," Otto continued, "overconfidence leads to underperformance."

Patrick rolled his eyes. "Stop making things up."

"I'm serious. The Dragons are leading the league in goals and assists and—"

Brock snorted. "Okay, okay. We know how good they are. Isn't there a statistic about how being scared of your opponent will get you beat?"

Riley was playing ping-pong against Kenji. "I ain't scared," Riley said with a sneer. "'Specially not of those barmy gits."

"I'm not scared either," Otto said. "Just realistic."

"Brock's right," I added. "We can't be afraid of them. We're good, too."

Kenji slammed a ping-pong ball on Riley's side so hard it bounced up and hit him on the nose. "We will fight them to the end and never surrender, like a fire blazing in our own hair."

I thought about that, had no idea what Kenji was talking about, and burst out laughing.

"I do not know what he is saying," said Dmitri in his heavy Russian accent as he watched Kenji twirl the paddle, pick up another ping-pong ball, and serve an ace. "But I think I agree."

"Geez," Riley said, as he whiffed another ball. "Wut did I do?"

"No mercy," Kenji said in a serious voice, causing us all to laugh harder.

The door opened, and Samantha popped her head in. "All right, guys. Let's get to bed. It's late, and I want you fresh for the game."

I headed to my room and tried to sleep but couldn't stop thinking about tomorrow. I tried to tell myself it was just another game, but a little voice in the back of my mind kept saying, *It isn't just another game. It's the finals of the Youth Prem. And you're playing against the number one team and a center mid who was better than you in the first game.*

I tried hard to shut that voice up. It wasn't doing me any favors. It only made my palms sweat and my stomach churn.

But there was another voice in my head, too. One that reminded me how hard we had fought to reach second place, everything we had overcome as a team, and my own struggles during the year. At one point, I hadn't even been sure I would finish the season or have a future in soccer.

You're a warrior, that voice said. *And no matter what, win or lose, you're going to fight to the end.*

I yawned and turned over, deciding to let the two voices talk to each other while I slept.

ENTRY #32

Knights versus Dragons: Second Joust

The next morning, I bounced out of bed, ready to play. After brushing my teeth and getting dressed, I glanced out of the window and saw gray skies with a ray of sunlight peeking through.

This was a home game. Noon kickoff. Before leaving my room, I clutched my lion's tooth necklace and stuck it in my bag for good luck.

After breakfast, we goofed off in the lounge, trying to relax, then moved to the field for a light warmup. Before I knew it, we were in the dressing room for Samantha's pre-game speech. When that was over, I took a deep breath and jogged through the tunnel with my teammates, stunned by all the people in the stands. I'd never seen them this full.

The atmosphere was electric.

The field was green and perfect, the lines crisp and white.

Let's go!

On the way to the field, we ran out beside the Dragons. As JoJo passed by Charlie, she said, "Hey, Chuck! Remember that time Leo rainbowed you at the Cage?"

The big Australian goalie shrugged. "Remember that time we smashed you this season?"

"It's gonna be worse this time," Fabio said. "A real beatdown."

"Three goals at least," Sebastian added with a smirk. "I guarantee it."

Other players started throwing barbs, so much that the referee blew his whistle and ordered us to separate.

"That's enough!" Samantha called out. "Play the game, Knights, or I'll sit you down."

The teams separated, but I could tell this was going to be war.

Samantha had chosen me as the captain. On my way to the center circle, I looked at the stands and saw Tig. I knew he couldn't root for us because we were playing his club, but I liked having him here.

José was the captain for the Dragons. "Good luck," he said, offering his hand.

I shook it. "You, too."

"Let's keep our teams calm."

"Deal."

José won the coin toss and chose to attack our goal. I jogged back and saw Diego, Aron, and Sebastian poised on the front line, ready to run. Every muscle in my body tensed as the whistle blew.

Game on!

The Dragons didn't waste any time. Diego kicked off to José, who worked the ball to Mikkel, the Danish right mid. After evading Otto's tackle, Mikkel chipped the ball over the defense, trying to lead Diego to the goal.

We scrambled to get back. Diego had lined up beside

Brock, staying onside. Now he burst forward, got a step ahead, and met Riley at the ball.

Diego threw his big shoulder into Riley, keeping him away, then took one dribble and passed to Aron, who was streaking in from the right, just ahead of Emile. On his first touch, Aron blasted a shot on goal. JoJo barely got a hand on it, jumping high to tip it over the crossbar.

Oh boy. Aron was going to be a problem. He was too much for Emile to handle on defense. But if we subbed in Kenji, we'd lose Emile's skill as an attacker.

Corner kick. Sebastian dropped his hand and whipped in a sizzling cross. Bodies flew everywhere. Diego rose high, but Brock won the battle and headed the ball out. When Duncan tried to clear it, Fabio stuck out a leg and blocked the kick. After a nifty stepover, the Italian midfielder took another shot, again forcing JoJo to make a tough save.

The Dragons kept up the pressure. Ten minutes went by, and I barely touched the ball. I spent all my time running back to help on defense and chasing José around the middle.

But at last I got a chance.

After another push by the Dragons, Riley tackled Sebastian so hard the Polish winger flew off his feet. He might have lost a few pimples. After dribbling forward, Riley fed me in the center.

I had my back to the ball. José was pushing up against me. I flicked the ball to my left and went in the same direction, using my body to shield José. In the past, I hadn't used that turn very much, because it relied on a strong base and shielding technique. But I realized, as I kept José off the ball with ease, that I was a different player now. The last time we met,

José seemed to have taken a big leap forward in his play and strength.

Now it was my turn.

As the Brazilian struggled to keep up, I surged ahead, the field opening up like a peeled onion. I saw Patrick poised to make a run and sent him the ball. It was a beautiful pass, leading him just right, but I'd had forgotten how fast Pedro, the fullback on Patrick's side, could run.

Almost no one beat Patrick to the ball. But this time, Pedro won the footrace by the thinnest of hairs. The Brazilian fullback poked the ball out of bounds, giving their defense time to set up.

"Here!" I cried, racing forward as Otto took the throw.

He gave me the ball. I danced to my right, narrowly avoiding a tackle by Fabio, and hit Dmitri in the middle. Our Russian striker let the ball go through his legs and spun, a tricky move that would have fooled most defenders.

But he was playing against Hans and Mateo. Neither took the bait. As Hans shouldered Dmitri to the side, causing him to stumble, Mateo cleared the ball halfway to Big Ben.

For a long time, that was the closest we got to their goal. Every time we came within spitting distance of the penalty box, Hans and Mateo closed us down like a steel door slamming shut. Only a few weak shots got through, which Charlie batted away like slow-moving balloons.

On the other end, Emile finally made a tackle on Aron and cleared the ball. I recovered it and swept my gaze across the field. Otto was covered, so I passed to Ajay. He was doing great, helping out on defense and making good passes. But this time, he left his pass to Marco a little short, and Mateo intercepted it. Without breaking stride, the Argentinian defender sent a one-touch pass down the left side of the field.

This was Sebastian's side. So far, Duncan had him under control, but the counterattack caught him off guard. Sebastian was very fast and won the race. He took one touch and sent a curving ball into the middle.

Diego raced towards it. This time, not even Riley could keep up, and Diego arrived first. He didn't bother taking a touch. He just slammed a perfect volley into the bottom left corner from ten yards out. JoJo barely had time to move.

After the goal, the tall Mexican striker jogged back, wagging a finger in the air. The home crowd fell silent. Diego rarely celebrated or trash talked. He just played his game and outscored everyone else.

The whistle blew to restart the game.

Down 1–0, we worked hard to level the score before halftime. Everyone surged forward. Coach Anderson barked encouragement, and Samantha windmilled her arms, urging us on.

Under pressure from Mikkel, Otto sent me a pass in midfield with José and Fabio right on top of me. They hounded me, and I worked hard not to lose the ball, spinning this way and that, using my body and arms to shield them. I kept dancing, faking one direction and moving the ball in another, pulling it back and rolling it to the side with the bottom of my foot. Eventually, I found a crack in their armor and slipped a pass to Ajay.

I darted forward. "Back to me!"

Ajay listened. He gave me the ball, and Hans stepped up. I kept pushing, making him think I was going to take him on my own. To be honest, I wasn't sure what I was going to do. Dmitri, Patrick, and Marco were all making runs, trying to get open.

Hans backpedaled, wary of my moves. I kept going, forcing him to commit. That opened up a gap in their defense. I slipped a pass on the ground to Marco, inches past Hans's diving leg.

Marco whipped the ball across the box to Patrick. As soon as he trapped it, Mateo was all over him. We didn't have time to wait. Their midfielders were racing back to help. "Here!" I cried, sprinting towards Patrick. He fed me the ball, and I rolled it back to Otto without looking, sensing he was making a run.

Once I made the pass, I turned and saw Otto's thick leg smack the ball right in the sweet spot. The shot was incredible, soaring towards the top right corner . . . but Charlie dove and gobbled it up.

What does it take to score on these guys?

Soon after, the halftime whistle blew. We hung our heads on the way to the locker room. Sure, we were only down 1–0, but they'd had the ball most of the half, and it seemed like a matter of time before they scored again.

"All right, Knights," Samantha said as we gathered in the dressing room, exhausted and gulping down water. "Not a bad first half. Keep those heads up! We're right there in the game. Tighten up those passes and keep the pressure on. I know Diego and Aron are tough, but remember, you don't have to steal the ball to win the battle. You just need to slow them down and let your teammates help out."

She clasped her hands behind her back and began to

pace in front of the table with the replica field. She paced for some time before she spoke, lips pursed, her gaze narrow and intense. "Real talk, Knights," she said finally. "As I said, you're playing well. But I need more belief out there. I need to see in your eyes, right now, that you think you can win this game. Remember last season? You *can* beat these guys. Forget the standings and the leading goal scorers and everything else. In one game of soccer, one *half*, anything can happen. You've come so far this year. Who wants to come in second place?"

"I don't," I said quietly.

"I'm sorry. I couldn't hear you very well."

"No one!" Brock roared. "We're gonna win this game!"

"That's better. Who else thinks we can win?"

This time, all of us shouted so loud I bet we woke up the royal family in Buckingham Palace.

Samantha pushed off the table. "I know you can. I see how good you are every day, and I know each and every one of you has a warrior spirit. Here's my coaching advice for the second half. It's not about tactics or positioning. We've prepared for that already. You know your jobs." She stepped closer to us, crossed her arms, and looked slowly around the group, meeting our eyes one by one. "I want you to go out there in the second half, play as hard as you can for forty-five minutes, and believe that you can win. That's it. You may not win the game. That's fine. We can't win everything all the time. No one does. But I want you to believe with all your hearts, as individuals and as a team, right now, that you can do it. I want you to walk out on that field for the second half and *believe*, Knights. Because you can win this title. You can beat these guys."

Brock leaped to his feet, threw a fist in the air, and roared, "*Knigggghhhts!*"

I jumped up next, followed by the rest of the team. We pumped our arms and shouted all the way out of the dressing room, causing the Dragons to look at us funny as they exited the tunnel looking calm and relaxed.

ENTRY #33

The Final: Part Two

Samantha's speech had given the whole team energy. Right before the whistle blew, I looked up and caught Tig's eye. He gave me a thumbs-up, and I dug in, ready to start the half.

For the first five minutes, we beat the Dragons to the ball all over the field. We just seemed to want it more. We won every duel and had three shots before they crossed half field.

After making another save, Charlie punted the ball to the center circle. I had been leading the attack and was caught too far ahead. But I started sprinting and managed to catch José while he was dribbling, forcing him to pass to Mikkel. I still didn't stop and pressured the Danish winger from behind. He tried to shield me off, but I fought through and stole the ball. Furious, he tried to steal it back, pushing and shoving and even trying to trip me. The ref raised the whistle but let it play out, seeing if I could gain an advantage.

Mikkel had kicked the back of my legs, causing me to stumble, but I tightened my core, regained my balance, and pushed forward. I could have taken the foul, but now we had numbers.

At the edge of my vision, I saw Otto making a run deep in enemy territory. I took a breath and launched a long, daring pass halfway across the field. The Dragons rushed to get back, caught by surprise.

As the ball fell to Otto, he chest-trapped it, spun, and played an excellent ball to Patrick, splitting two defenders. Patrick raced forward, looping behind Pedro, and slashed the ball across the front of the goal. Dmitri had pulled back, drawing Mateo away. Marco was racing inside. As Charlie came out of the goal, Marco launched his body forward, diving in front of Hans and reaching the ball with his foot an instant before Charlie. The shot grazed the Australian goalie's outstretched leg, kept going, and rolled into the back of the net.

Tie game!

As we celebrated, I saw, in the corner of my eye, the Dragons coach shouting at his players. Whatever he said, it seemed to wake them up. They came at us hard and kept up the pressure.

After José received a pass in midfield, he flicked the ball behind his leg to Fabio, who made a quick one-touch pass to Aron. Emile was there to defend. As the pass came in, the big Swiss winger pretended to trap the ball, then took a long touch down the wing and blew past Emile.

Uh-oh.

Aron raced down the sideline with a full head of steam, leaving Emile in the dust. Brock raced over to cut him off. Aron started to cross the ball, then pushed the ball past Brock as well. It was a clever play, because everyone in the stadium thought Aron would cross to Diego.

Brock shifted his position faster than someone his size should move, but Aron got a step on him anyway, and kept dribbling. This forced Riley to leave Diego and block Aron's path to the goal. Riley arrived in time to defend, but this time Aron did cut it back, a simple pass on the ground to Diego.

The right foot of the talented Mexican striker connected with the ball and creamed it towards the bottom left corner. JoJo dove and stretched out . . .

And saved the shot!

As she smacked it to the side, my heart soared, but before I had time to celebrate, Sebastian raced in, half a step ahead of Duncan, and poked the rebound into the goal.

I groaned and put my hands against my head.

Just like that, the Dragons were up again.

It was deflating. We had worked so hard to get even, but they had flipped a switch and gone to another level.

Were they just better than us?

Brock slammed a hand against the goalpost. I ran back and said, "Forget about it. You were worried about Diego."

He snarled. "Get up there and work some magic, Yank. They're not getting through again."

After the goal, Samantha substituted Kenji for Emile. It was a smart choice. Aron was killing Emile on the wing. We had to slow him down.

The substitution helped, but the Dragons have lots of weapons. Duncan had his hands full with Sebastian. Brock and Riley had to work together to slow down Diego. In midfield, I was holding my own against José, even winning the battle, but Fabio and Mikkel were almost as good.

And Aron was giving Kenji a hard time, threatening to break free every time he touched the ball. I knew we had to keep more possession and press the attack. If we didn't, our defense would be overwhelmed.

JoJo made a save and slung the ball to me. I shifted left,

getting José to bite, then passed to Ajay. "Back to me!" I yelled, overlapping him on the sideline.

Ajay chose Otto instead. I raced back to the center. Mikkel tried to slide tackle Otto, but my friend's nimble feet evaded the attempt and pushed the ball to Patrick. With his red hair flying, Patrick spun around Pedro and kept running, finally getting the better of him. It was a great move, but Hans stepped up to stop Patrick's momentum.

After dancing near the edge of the box, Patrick passed to Dmitri, who faked a pass to Marco and cut back for a shot. But Mateo read his attempt and tackled him hard, sending Dmitri to the ground.

The referee waved his arms. No foul.

Back the other way it went. Mateo passed to José in the middle. I read the play but couldn't get there in time. José knew I was right behind him and sent a one-touch ball to Fabio. I chased after him. Fabio chipped a pass down the line, letting Sebastian run.

Long limbs flying, Sebastian reached the ball first and cut inside. But Duncan had stayed with him and threw himself into a slide tackle that barely caught the ball and knocked it aside.

"Yes, Duncan!" Samantha yelled. "Great hustle!"

Somehow Duncan bounced to his feet and recovered the ball. Under heavy pressure, he passed to Ajay, who had Fabio on his back. Instead of shielding and waiting for help, Ajay panicked and tried a pass to me that José intercepted.

In the blink of an eye, José passed ahead to Diego, who made a beautiful flick to Aron on the wing. Aron sprinted forward with Kenji on his heels. Just before Aron got off the shot, Kenji dove and blocked it, sending the ball out of bounds.

Corner kick.

Kenji adjusted his headband and marked Aron, sticking to him like a shadow. Brock pushed against Diego, and Riley battled with Fabio for position. I ran back, wiping sweat from my eyes and gasping for air. I glanced at the clock. Ten minutes to go. If the game ended in a tie, the Dragons would win the title. Somehow we had to score at least two goals in the last few minutes. The way things were going, it didn't seem possible.

José and I bumped and shouldered each other in the box. I got the better of him and crowded him back, but it didn't matter. The ball flew past us, and Brock headed it out.

I thought we were safe, but Hans was waiting for the loose ball. He had pushed ahead and muscled Ajay to the side. Hans sent the ball right back into the box, where Diego barely missed a half-volley.

Whew. Close one. I let out a breath and ran back into position.

On the next play, Pedro intercepted a pass and played a long ball to Aron, who tried a shot that JoJo barely saved.

They were really pounding us. We couldn't seem to hold possession, especially with Emile on the bench.

Five minutes to go.

After Diego narrowly missed another shot, I sprinted back to help out on the goal kick, calling for the ball. Enough was enough. We had to try something different.

Brock kicked it to me. I held off José, passed to Otto, and darted forward. "Here!"

Otto sent it back. Fabio slid over to cut me off. I noticed

Ajay was open and curled the ball around Fabio, hitting Ajay on the fly. Both Otto and I pushed forward, trying to get numbers, but Ajay's touch got away from him again, allowing Fabio to steal it. The Dragons knew that Ajay was playing in place of Goran and were taking advantage of his side.

Fabio raced down the sideline, but Ajay stayed with him, working hard to get back, then sliding in to steal the ball. Just as I and everyone else thought he was the weak link, Ajay proved us wrong with his hustle. Even better, he jumped up, beat Fabio to the loose ball, and kicked it ahead, using his speed to get downfield before Fabio could catch him.

Now we had numbers. Ajay passed ahead to Marco, and the Colombian winger didn't waste any time. With a perfect first touch, he cut straight towards the goal, forcing Mateo to slide over. When the Argentinian defender went for the tackle, Marco slipped the ball to the middle, where I was waiting.

But so was Hans. The big German came right at me, filling my line of vision. I could smell his sweat and see the veins bulging in his thick neck.

Both Dmitri and Patrick were covered. I could swing the ball back to Otto, but that would kill our breakaway. It was time to take a chance. I faked a flick, getting Hans to open up, and poked the ball through his legs. The nutmeg worked, but that was the easy part. Now I had to get around him. In the past, there was no way I would have squeezed past him when we were this close. A nutmeg works best when you have momentum and room to move. Hans was right on top of me, about to plow me over. But I used all my strength and surged past him, pushing off his body with my right arm, keeping it low to avoid a foul. As I turned the corner, Hans bumped me with his hip, enough to send me flying. But on my way to the ground, I reached out with a leg and flicked the ball forward, just past another defender.

My flick landed right on the penalty spot. Dmitri darted past his defender, barely staying onside, and slammed the ball at the goal. Charlie dove to his right, his big body flying through the air, but he was a split-second too late.

Splash went the net.

Tie game.

I jumped to my feet, joining Patrick as he barreled into Dmitri to celebrate. Within moments, the entire team had arrived, and the Russian striker was grinning ear to ear.

"Get back!" Samantha cried. "We need another one!"

She was right. We separated and raced back to our side of the field. As the referee blew the whistle, the Dragons dug in, grim faced and ready.

Diego looked as if he wanted to score all by himself. After kicking off to José, the Mexican striker rushed downfield like a charging rhino. José tried to pass back to him, but I read the play and stole the ball. José changed directions, trying to cut me off, but I snuck past him and led Marco down the wing. A defender was there, so Marco passed to Ajay, who tried a long cross to Patrick. I held my breath as my friend took off, jumped high in the air, let out a loud, "Kee-yaii!" and snapped the ball towards the near post.

It was a great header, but Charlie was ready. He made the save look easy and slung the ball downfield, starting a counterattack.

Aron trapped the ball, held off Kenji with an arm, and found Mikkel streaking forward. As the Danish winger cut inside, aiming straight for the goal, Brock ran over and slide tackled him. This time Brock didn't miss, sending the ball and the player flying out of bounds.

As Mikkel called for a foul, Brock flung up his hands, whipping the crowd into a frenzy.

Back and forth it went. Both teams gave everything they had. As badly as each side wanted to win, no one wanted to make a mistake this close to the end of the game. It was nerve-wracking. We had to take risks to get a goal, but if we missed a pass or had the ball stolen, it could lead to a counterattack and a third goal by the Dragons that would seal their victory.

Didn't matter. I had to play my game and go for goal. I'd never forgive myself if I didn't take every chance I had.

The problem was, I might not get another one. With two minutes to go, the Dragons had the ball in midfield and weren't giving it up. Fabio and Mikkel and José were making triangles and keeping possession. I finally managed to knock the ball away, but Hans was there to recover it. He tried a long pass to Diego, but Riley swooped in like an eagle and stole it.

Sebastian ran over to challenge him. Riley shoved him off and dribbled upfield, his rattail swinging. As Fabio raced over, Riley passed to Ajay, who got stuck near the sideline. One of the Dragons stripped the ball and made a quick pass to Sebastian.

No no no. Duncan had pressed forward to help Ajay and was caught out of position. Now Sebastian was all alone on the wing and surging towards the goal.

Riley slid over. After hesitating, Sebastian crossed to Aron on the other side. Brock didn't give him any room, but

Aron made a tricky one-touch chest pass to Mikkel, who had sprinted forward to help, leaving Otto lagging behind. I could tell Otto was winded and badly needed a sub.

Mikkel took the pass and, with one smooth touch, passed by Brock and entered the penalty box. Diego was calling for the ball, but Riley had him covered. After another dribble, Mikkel hit a curving shot towards the top right corner. I thought for sure it was a goal—right until JoJo leaped high and made an acrobatic save, somehow landing with the ball in her arms.

Samantha jumped up and down on the sideline. "Great save, Jo! Now *push!*"

We were in extra time now, with less than a minute to go. JoJo whipped the ball out to Kenji, who passed ahead to Otto. He was gassed, so he gave it to me near half field, even though José was coming fast. He was so close that we were going to reach the ball almost at the same time.

I didn't have time to plan. I just knew I had to keep possession. As the ball came in, I did a hocus pocus, pulling the ball behind my left leg with my right foot, then whipping it forward into the space past José. I jumped over his outstretched foot, pushed through his grab at my jersey, and kept going. The crowd went nuts over the move.

I pressed forward but we didn't have numbers. The Dragons had all their defenders back, and none of my teammates were open. But I had to keep moving. I shifted left, into some open space. Fabio stayed with me. Even if I beat him, Hans and Mateo were lurking, ready to shut me down.

In the corners, Patrick and Marco were waiting for a pass, and Dmitri was poised on Mateo's shoulder, but everyone was marked tight. I had to try something.

Who should I go to?

After a slight hesitation, I sent the ball to Patrick. I trusted him a little more than the others in crunch time. When he received my pass, he took a touch deeper into Dragon territory, trying to get open for a cross. Pedro stayed with him. This might be the last play of the game. If Pedro stole the ball, I doubted we would get another chance.

There was no time to ball watch. I sucked in a breath and made a run, curling around Hans and racing towards the edge of the penalty box. As I arrived, I saw Pedro strip the ball from Patrick, and my heart sank.

Time was almost up. All Pedro had to do was launch the ball downfield.

As his leg swung back, somehow, incredibly, Patrick came from behind, threw his body forward, and blocked the pass. Then he flipped to his feet, rolled the ball back, spun around Pedro, and darted towards the end line.

Yes, Patrick!

Pedro recovered, but not before Patrick managed to whip off a cross.

His effort wasn't perfect. In fact, it wasn't even a good cross. Patrick had been under too much pressure. The ball wasn't headed towards Dmitri or Marco or anywhere close to the goal. In fact, it was sailing over my head, towards the outer edge of the penalty box. In the corner of my eye, I didn't see any of my other teammates close enough to make a good play. The cross was going to sail harmlessly to the feet of a Dragon.

There was only one possible play on the ball, and it wasn't a good one. But I knew I had to take it, despite the tiny chance of success.

As the cross sailed in, I leaped as high as I could, throwing my body in the air. Time seemed to stand still as I kept my back parallel to the ground, chest facing the sky, watching the ball as it came in. My timing had to be perfect. Even if I pulled this off, Charlie would probably make the save.

The ball soared overhead. I tightened my core and scissored my legs in midair, striking the ball as it went past, changing its direction with a powerful bicycle kick. The same kick I had practiced over and over during our night sessions for months. This time, I struck the ball with the top of my right foot, smacking it in the sweet spot, and the ball took off like a bolt of lightning. I landed hard on my back, losing my wind as I sacrificed my body for the shot.

But I had enough strength to turn on the ground and watch the ball scream over the heads of the defenders, glance off Charlie's outstretched fingertips, strike the goalpost near the top right corner, and bounce over the goal line and into the back of the net.

ENTRY #34

Mirror Mirror

The whistle blew, signaling the end of the game.

We had just won the Youth Prem.

My teammates mobbed me, but I still hadn't caught my breath from the hard fall. I lay gasping on the ground like a fish out of water, trying to speak as Brock lifted me in the air and shouted our team name.

"Did that just happen?" Patrick said, plucking at his red hair as I regained my wind. "Did you just score on a bicycle kick at the last second? Luckabucka, Leo, that was in*sane!*"

The crowd was still going wild. I walked to the bench in a daze, barely able to believe it myself.

Samantha had a huge smile on her face. She high-fived everyone, then shepherded us back on the field to shake hands with the Dragons. "Nothing but class," she warned. "Be humble in victory."

"I better stay here then," Riley said, then threw up his hands when Samantha glared at him. "Wut? I'm kidding."

As we formed a line, I noticed Tig looking at me from the first row. He pointed a finger right at me, then shook his head and mouthed *Wow*.

I hadn't forgotten the first game, when the refs and the coaches had to separate the teams. But this time, the Dragons went through with lowered heads, and there weren't any problems.

"Good game," Aron said as I passed him. "You killed us out there."

"You, too."

José was next in line. He leaned in close and said, in his Brazilian accent, "They made a big mistake not choosing you at the Academy, Leo. A big mistake."

I grinned and moved on, exchanging fist bumps with lots of my old friends: Sergi, Conor, Dayo, and Fabio.

"I'm really sick of you, Leo," Hans said with a sigh as we slapped hands.

Charlie and Mateo and Diego mumbled *good game* but wouldn't look me in the eye. Neither would Sebastian, who had guaranteed three goals in the game. That had happened, just not for his team.

Riley and everyone else stayed calm and obeyed Samantha's order. After the handshake line, our team walked off the field with the cheers of the home crowd ringing in our ears. On my way to the bench, Coach Anderson caught up with me.

"I have to say, Leo, I was wrong about you. I knew you were talented, but I didn't know you had so much . . . grit."

"Thanks, Coach."

"Really great season. Keep proving me wrong."

"I'll try."

Right before we left the field, I saw Goran staring at me from the other end of the bench. He didn't look angry, but he didn't look happy either. I wasn't sure what he was thinking. I paused and stared back at him, wondering if he would say something or approach me, but he never did. After a long moment, I gave him a single nod, my way of saying I didn't have any more hard feelings. He did the same, then turned and headed towards the dressing room.

⚽ ⚽ ⚽

We celebrated all day long, threw another pizza party, and stayed up most of the night, reliving the entire season and especially the final game.

The next day, Samantha surprised us at breakfast by carrying in a large trophy with *U14 Youth Premier League Champions* engraved on the front, along with the year. We all gathered around it, speechless at how big it was and what it represented. Not in our wildest dreams, when we were stuck at the bottom of the table for much of last season, could we have imagined we would win the Youth Prem.

⚽ ⚽ ⚽

I wished I had more time to celebrate with my teammates, but my flight home left the next day. I said goodbye to everyone, including Tig and Samantha, and knew I'd see them all soon.

What would next season bring?

I was moving up to the U16s and knew that would be a big change. I would be a year younger than many of the players and would have to fight for my position all over again. But at least I'd be with John and Eddy and the rest of my old teammates.

Or would I? Would someone else transfer to another team? Or get injured or cut from the squad?

What would the new players be like? What new challenges would rise up for us to overcome?

Could we win the title again next year, in a higher division? It would be really tough. The Dragons would be itching for revenge, and maybe another team would step up.

In the Prem, you never knew what might happen.

⚽ ⚽ ⚽

When I returned to Middleton, my friends already knew we had won the league. Carlos and Dennis were kicking a ball in my front yard when my dad and I got back from the airport. Before I had a chance to go inside, my friends made me give them a full description of the final game, goal by goal. When I told them about the bicycle kick, Carlos didn't even believe me.

"Shut up, Leo. You didn't do a bicycle kick to win the Youth Prem."

"I did."

"It was probably like, you know, a half-bicycle or something. A unicycle kick."

"Nope. It was a real one. I landed flat on my back and lost my breath."

"You are just not even serious."

I laughed. "I promise. It happened."

Dennis put his hands against his head in disbelief, and Carlos rolled his eyes. "You are so lucky. You were probably trying to pass the ball to the corner."

⚽ ⚽ ⚽

My two friends spent the night and most of the next day at my house. After they left, and I had some time to myself, I lay on my back on my bed, a little tired from all the traveling and the late night with my friends.

I was excited about the summer. I had weeks to hang out and do nothing. Samantha hadn't mentioned the Tournament of Champions, and I wondered if we would travel around Europe again.

Little did I know at this point—here's a sneak preview for you—that an even greater challenge was waiting for me.

But I'll tell you about that soon enough.

For now, I was looking forward to a good night's sleep and long days of doing nothing except playing pickup with my friends, destroying them at FIFA, hanging at the pool, and having sleepovers. I'd read some manga and watch some movies at the theater. There would also be plenty of pizza and banana pancakes, I promise you that.

From the corner, I heard a little hiss coming from Messi's cage. That meant he was upset about something. I raised up on my elbows and saw him glaring at me.

"I know, I know. I've been ignoring you."

I walked over, fed him dinner, gave him plenty of attention, and watched him strut to the top of his fake tree with a satisfied expression.

"Can you believe we won the league?" I said. "I still can't."

He didn't seem very interested.

After stroking his neck for a while, I got ready for bed. Just before I slipped on a T-shirt and turned out the lights, I stood in front of the mirror attached to my door, my lion's tooth necklace resting against my bare chest. I put my arms over my head and flexed my biceps, trying to see how much muscle I had gained.

"You see that, Messi? Huh? Huh? You see that?"

When I glanced back at him, he was busy gnawing on a leaf.

I frowned and turned back to the mirror. I couldn't really tell if my biceps were any bigger, so I kept flexing in different positions, trying to see if any of my muscles had grown. I thought my triceps might have swelled a bit, and my forearms, and when I squeezed my chest really hard, I thought I could see some pecs coming in. Or was I imagining that?

"What do you think, Messi? Can you tell?"

As I walked over to his cage, holding the chest pose, someone knocked on the door and turned the knob. I jumped three feet in the air and stopped posing. "Uh, yeah?"

Ginny poked her head in. "Dad says brush your teeth before bed."

"Yeah, okay. Knock next time. And go away."

She stuck out her tongue, and I rolled my eyes. Our team wins the Youth Prem and I still have to deal with my little sister.

After she left, I flexed one more time for Messi, this time making a fist and showing him the side of my arm. It took me a while to get his attention, but finally he turned, watched me with a bored expression, and then walked away.

I turned back to the mirror and stared at myself for a long moment. Then I shook my head and laughed.

**COMING SOON!
THE ACADEMY V: CUP OF NATIONS**

To stay up to date on the Academy Series and other stories by T.Z. Layton, it's best to join his New Release Newsletter:

subscribepage.com/tzlaytonbooks

Acknowledgments

Thanks once again to my fantastic cover designer Rob Ball, my eagle-eyed editing team (David Downing, Meredith Tennant, and Jaye Manus) and my wonderful advance readers: Zara, Ella, John, and Deborah. I'd also like to thank all the readers, parents, teachers, and librarians who have helped spread the word for the Academy series. Truly, this author is humbled beyond words. Finally, I'm very grateful to the 2 Seas Agency for their tireless efforts in bringing the adventures of Leo and his friends to young readers around the globe.

About the Author

T.Z. LAYTON is bestselling author Layton Green's pen name for books aimed at younger readers. The author's novels have been nominated for many awards, translated into multiple languages, and optioned for film. The author is also a soccer dad, youth coach, former collegiate player, and lifelong fan of the beautiful game.

Word of mouth is crucial to the success of any author. If you enjoyed Leo's adventures, please consider leaving an honest review on Goodreads, Amazon, Barnes & Noble, or another book site, even if it's only a line or two. (Note: if you're under 13, please ask a parent to help you.)

You can visit T.Z. on Facebook, Goodreads, or at tzlaytonbooks.com for additional information on the author, his works, and more.